Laws banning exchanges of widely desired goods or services (such as drugs, abortion, or gambling) often create more problems than they solve. As the authors of VICTIMLESS CRIMES stress, whether or not to legislate in these areas is an urgent social and intellectual question for our time.

Edwin M. Schur, an outstanding leader in the field of criminology, explains why attempts to legislate morality fail to stop "socially unacceptable" forms of behavior. Hugo Adam Bedau, a well-known philosopher, challenges the basic concept of victimless crimes and the moral inconsistency in social attitudes toward these controversial problems.

Approaching the topic from different vantage points, they discuss such aspects as:

- The human, social, and constitutional costs of criminalizing such behavior
- The complexity of making moral and legal judgments in these situations
- The search for general principles that should underlie criminal legislation

VICTIMLESS CRIMES offers a unique cross-disciplinary analysis of a major public policy issue in America today.

Chairman of the
author of seven
and Society: A
ocial and Legal
onintervention:

ssor of Philoso-
University. He
ice-Hall); *The*
dience: Theory
ent volumes of
hy and Public

EDWIN M. SCHUR is Professor of Sociology and Chairman of the Department at New York University. He is the author of seven books, including *Crimes Without Victims, Law and Society: A Sociological View; Our Criminal Society; The Social and Legal Sources of Crime in America; and Radical Nonintervention: Rethinking the Delinquency Problem.*

HUGO ADAM BEDAU is Austin B. Fletcher Professor of Philosophy and Chairman of the Department at Tufts University. He is the editor of *Justice and Equality* (Prentice-Hall), *The Death Penalty in America,* and *Civil Disobedience: Theory and Practice,* and a contributing author to recent volumes of essays sponsored by the Society for Philosophy and Public Affairs.

VICTIMLESS CRIMES

VICTIMLESS CRIMES

TWO SIDES
OF A
CONTROVERSY

Edwin M. Schur
and
Hugo Adam Bedau

Prentice-Hall, Inc. *Englewood Cliffs, N. J.*
A SPECTRUM BOOK

Library of Congress Cataloging in Publication Data

SCHUR, EDWIN M
  Victimless crimes.

  (A Spectrum Book)
  Includes bibliographies.
  1. Crimes without victims. 2. Criminal law.
I. Bedau, Hugo Adam. II. Title.
HV6705.S385   364.1   74–18255
ISBN 0–13–941690–0
ISBN 0–13–941682–X (pbk.)

10 9 8 7 6 5 4 3 2 1

PRENTICE-HALL INTERNATIONAL, INC. (*London*)
PRENTICE-HALL OF AUSTRALIA PTY. LTD. (*Sydney*)
PRENTICE-HALL OF CANADA LTD. (*Toronto*)
PRENTICE-HALL OF INDIA PRIVATE LIMITED (*New Delhi*)
PRENTICE-HALL OF JAPAN, INC. (*Tokyo*)

ACKNOWLEDGMENTS

Quotations from *The Limits of the Criminal Sanction* by Herbert L. Packer are used by kind permission of Stanford University Press.

The excerpt from the article "No Penalty Urged in Victimless Crimes" by Paul Montgomery, which appeared in *The New York Times* on January 28, 1973, is reprinted by permission. © 1973 by The New York Times Company.

CONTENTS

CONTENTS

PREFACE

The idea of doing this book first arose when one of us (Bedau) sent the other a paper critically analyzing the concept of victimless crime—which he had originally prepared for presentation at a conference in Israel. Particularly since the recipient (Schur) already had in mind the desirability of up-dating and stating in more general form the argument he had earlier advanced in *Crimes Without Victims* (1965), we thought that several purposes might be served by putting together a short volume reflecting our quite different perspectives on this topic.

For both scholars and the general public, questions relating to the scope and limits of the substantive criminal law have occasioned much controversy. Recently, in the face of an apparent trend toward decriminalization, discussion of these issues has taken on a new urgency. As various statutory proscriptions increasingly come to be scrutinized—in moral, legal, and sociological terms—it is vitally important that all relevant arguments, evidence, and interpretations should be fully aired. We make no attempt in this short book to provide encyclopedic coverage of this entire area—as the wealth of recent literature shows, the subject is now beyond the scope of any one volume to treat in thorough detail—rather, we present an overview of the debate as seen from (our particular versions of) a philosophical and a sociological perspective. Each of us has found a considerable challenge in the outlook of the other, and we believe the result is an unusual cross-disciplinary focus on a common set of policy issues rarely examined in this way. Hopefully, this combination of viewpoints will prove useful to others in trying to come to grips with the complexities of the victimless crime controversy; to students and scholars in law, philosophy, and sociology and perhaps other disciplines as well and also to the concerned general reader.

It will at once become apparent that the material in this volume does not neatly fit any predetermined "debate" format. Scholarly disagreement, such as will be found in our views, is rarely best presented in neatly circumscribed pro and con terms. Besides disagreeing on a number of specific facets of the problem, we tend toward rather different conceptions of how the problem ought to be framed in the first place. Accordingly, and to maintain the integrity of our diverse standpoints, we have drawn up quite independently our two initial essays— which appear in a form that projects rather than conceals these differences. At the same time, we have made no attempt there in the interest of controversy to artificially sharpen the contrasts in our overall policy outlooks. Following these general opening statements, each in turn comments on the other's argument, and these commentaries should highlight still further the nature and extent of our agreements and disagreements.

Our primary aim is quite simply to stimulate discussion and analysis of an area we both believe should be of great intellectual and social concern. Hopefully, readers will come to share our conviction regarding the importance of these questions and will find our ideas helpful in formulating or reassessing their own positions on the intellectual and public policy issues involved.

Edwin M. Schur

Hugo Adam Bedau

VICTIMLESS CRIMES

A
SOCIOLOGIST'S
VIEW

THE
CASE
FOR
ABOLITION

by EDWIN M. SCHUR

I
INTRODUCTION

It seems almost an American tradition to be excessively sanguine regarding the ability of the criminal law to solve social problems. Indeed, many Americans are overly quick to define as social problems any and all behavior patterns that offend or otherwise displease them. These tendencies have gotten us into a lot of trouble. They have led to gravely distorted priorities in the formulation and implementation of public policy, and have caused us inadvertently to produce new and unnecessary social harms. They have, in short, made matters worse rather than better.

Because of the unintended consequences of earlier policy decisions, there is a growing recognition that the criminal process is "an extraordinarily difficult and costly method of social control," and further that "the criminal sanction, inflicting as it does a unique combination of stigma and loss of liberty, should be resorted to only sparingly in a society that regards itself as free and open." (Packer, 1968, pp. 249–250) It is not possible to consider, in this brief essay, why we have for so long ignored the caveats of numerous legal philosophers. Certainly, our efforts to control human behavior through criminal legislation have been motivated at least in part by the desire to achieve ends and maximize values that many have believed to be essential for social well-being. Yet major changes in our society are compelling reassessment of basic goals as well as of the various means by which we might seek to attain them. As empirical data and realistic analysis replace misinformation and stereotyped thinking, neither the long-standing existence of a criminal statute nor a majority adherence to the norms and values it seeks to uphold is likely to be accepted as sufficient justification for maintaining it. More often, the test is whether, on balance and all things considered, the law serves useful social purposes. And in making this judgment, the informed citizen as well as the legal or sociological specialist now looks primarily not at its professed aims but rather at its real consequences—whether, and if so how, it affects human behavior and influences social situations.

During the past two decades there has been a striking trend toward reducing the scope of the substantive criminal law. Without question a major impetus for this development was provided by the report of the Wolfenden Committee, published in 1957. This governmental commission, charged with evaluating Britain's laws on homosexuality and prostitution, is probably best known for its recommendation that private homosexual acts between consenting adults ought not be subject to criminal penalty. Its major contribution, however, lay in eloquently asserting the advisability of society's placing but limited reliance on the criminal law. Arguing that such law should aim only at preserving public order and decency, protecting individuals from offensive and injurious behavior, and guarding against exploitation and corruption (particularly of those who are especially vulnerable), the Committee stated: "Unless a deliberate attempt is to be made by society, acting through the agency of the law, to equate the sphere of crime with that of sin, there must remain a realm of private morality and immorality which is, in brief and crude terms, not the law's business. To say this is not to condone or encourage private immorality." ([Wolfenden] Committee, *Report,* 1957.)

Although the Wolfenden Report ignited a considerable (and continuing) debate among legal scholars—some aspects of which we will be returning to below—the Committee's basic position, favoring limited application of the law, has rapidly gained adherents. In the United States alone, numerous governmental commissions, legal advisory bodies, and civic and professional organizations, have urged reducing the scope of criminal legislation—either in general or with respect to one or more specific spheres of conduct. Individual lawyers, judges, legislators, and even prosecutors and police officials, have condemned unwieldy crime laws, as have spokesmen for medical, social welfare, and other professional groups whose work often is affected by them. Legislatures in some American jurisdictions have "taken off the books" proscriptions previously embodied in their criminal codes; the most significant of such revisions has been that of the laws relating to abortion, which in some states have undergone a dramatic shift over the past ten years. (Lader, 1973)

The recent trend toward de-criminalization, and the controversy surrounding it, have primarily involved those borderline areas frequently referred to as "crimes without victims." (Schur, 1965) Since the meaning and applications of that term have become matters of considerable dispute, it may be helpful at the outset to define the concept and to highlight very generally its possible usefulness. Victimless crimes are created when we attempt to ban through criminal legislation the exchange between willing partners of strongly desired goods or services. The "offense" in such a situation, then, consists of a consensual transaction—one person gives or sells another person something he or she wants. Abortion, the sale of illicit drugs, illegal gambling, the sale of pornography, prostitution, and indeed virtually all proscribed sexual behavior involving willing partners (laws against homosexual acts being the most notable case in point), are major examples.

Of course there must have been reasons for our having defined such behaviors as criminal. Indeed, many persons would contend that these situations do involve victimization. The drug addict, they would argue, is a victim of his condition; the prostitute is victimized by her situation; some would assert even that the fetus is a victim in the case of abortion. As Richard Quinney has perceptively noted, in one sense all crimes must have victims: "Acts, in fact, are defined as criminal because someone or something is conceived of as a victim. . . . A 'victimless' crime can only be one that is defined after the fact by an outside observer." (Quinney, 1972, p. 315) This comment, at least by implication, highlights the impossibility of neatly resolving, for once and for all, the diverging assessments regarding victimization. These assessments are not simply empirical ones; on the contrary, they must inevitably involve value judgments and reflect the value hierarchies of the assessors. Just as an assertion of victimlessness represents a social definition imposed from "outside," so too does an assertion that in a given situation there is a victim (whether it be a specifiable individual, or society at large). The more cogent question, then, is not really whether a given behavior *is* a crime, but rather whether it *should be treated as such*.

There is, however, another sense in which these transactional "crimes" are victimless—and it is one of overriding significance. Quite simply, the persons involved in exchanging (illicit) goods and services *do not see themselves* as victims. They are, therefore, most unlikely to complain to the police. In the absence of such complainants, the difficulties involved in obtaining evidence necessary to enforce these laws are (as we shall see in some detail) virtually insurmountable. It is not necessary, at this point, to consider the issue of whether we may be entitled morally to view another individual as victimized when he does not so view himself. What must, however, be emphasized most emphatically is that attempts to proscribe such exchanges through the criminal law invariably have certain objective consequences (those pertaining to enforcement, and others—to be detailed below) *regardless of* any imputations of victimization that may be made by outside observers.

It is true that no criminal law ever has an absolute grounding in universally accepted and adhered-to norms. As a leading criminologist once aptly noted: "When the mores are adequate laws are unnecessary; when the mores are inadequate, the laws are ineffective." (Sutherland and Cressey, 1960, p. 11) Furthermore, criminal laws often may be thought to have important symbolic and educational value even when they compel less than complete adherence. But unless the overall effect of criminal legislation is to influence behavior in the desired direction, grave question may arise concerning its justification. The debate about whether one can "legislate morality" involves more than abstract moral dilemmas, for specific kinds of social situations vary greatly in the extent to which they can be legally controlled. Consensual transactions are remarkably resistant to such control, especially when the legislative proscription aims at behavior likely to occur in relatively "private" settings. Enforcement effectiveness is maximized when the offense is not only reportable by a complainant but also has high public visibility; it is weakest when the "crime" is not only victimless but shielded from public scrutiny. (Duster, 1970, pp. 23–28)

As we shall see, a number of broad developments have contributed to or reinforced the trend toward de-criminalization. Central to these developments has been a growing impatience with euphemism and with abstract (and sometimes hypocritical) moralizing. Americans are displaying a heightened critical awareness with respect to the substance and administration of the criminal law; they are increasingly prepared to question the value of a law once they discover that it does not work out well in practice. This process has been facilitated in recent years as sophisticated investigations by social scientists, legal analysts, and governmental commissions, have produced a more comprehensive and accurate understanding than existed earlier both of the operation of victimless crime laws and of the behaviors they seek to control. To a considerable extent, past support for these laws often rested on misinformation regarding the nature and ramifications of the proscribed acts. As a result unsubstantiated assertions of the "horrible consequences" likely to follow from de-criminalization frequently went unchallenged. This is not longer possible.

The growing objection to victimless crime laws is not based solely on their unenforceability. Beyond their failure to achieve desired ends, such laws often appear to increase or worsen social harms rather than reduce them. Although the extent to which these laws give rise to one or another of these harms varies, a general pattern clearly does emerge. Attempts to apply them occupy a large part of the time, energy, and money available for all law-enforcement activity. They force the police to adopt legally and morally questionable investigative techniques, and yet even these methods prove largely ineffective to curb the proscribed behavior. Actually the attempt to ban these transactions encourages and reinforces the growth of an illicit traffic and raises the price of the goods and services in question. As we shall see, some of these laws produce secondary crime (i.e., other than the proscribed behavior itself), and all create new "criminals"—many of whom are otherwise law-abiding individuals. Victimless crime laws tend to degrade decent human beings, and invariably their administration is arbitrary and discriminatory; certain segments of society feel their impact a great deal more than others. The largely discretionary nature of their enforcement, along with the other key features of victimless crime situations, invites corruption and exploitation and may throw the entire system of criminal justice into disrepute.

Perhaps particularly because of the way in which they affect crime priorities, these laws not only fail in their specific areas of intended control; they significantly color the entire sphere of crime policy. Recognizing this, two close students of crime recently asserted:

> . . . we must strip off the moralistic excrescences of our criminal justice system so that it may concentrate on the essential. The prime function of the criminal law is to protect our persons and our property; these purposes are now engulfed in a mass of other distracting, inefficiently performed, legislative duties. When the criminal law invades the spheres of private morality and social welfare, it exceeds its proper limits at the cost of neglecting its primary tasks. This unwarranted extension is expensive, ineffective, and criminogenic. (Morris and Hawkins, 1970, p. 2)

While documentation of these points has increased rapidly in recent years, evidence (for example, of deterrent impact) that might provide some counterbalancing justification for the laws remains negligible. Sometimes, supporters of these laws argue as though the wealth of empirical data now available concerning their operation were somehow simply irrelevant to the moral issues posed by such efforts to control offending behavior. Yet this argument, that looks to the "law on the books" (and seems to assume it to be fully enforceable and beneficial), rather than to the "law in action," is extremely misleading. To imply that the relevant value choice is between abolishing these behaviors and permitting them to exist is to engage in the most self-deceptive kind of wishful thinking. The more cogent issue is not whether we approve or disapprove of the behaviors in question, but rather whether we approve or disapprove of efforts to curb them through the criminal law. These have not been hypothetical efforts (although admittedly some proposed alternatives may be). They are real efforts that have had objective and demonstrable consequences. To attempt to make a judgment on them without taking into account the weight of the available evidence would be to act in a morally irresponsible manner.

II
COSTS OF CRIMINALIZING

ENFORCEMENT

Some years ago, a perceptive legal analyst described the American system of criminal justice as, "a weary Atlas upon whose shoulders we have heaped a crushing burden of responsibilities relating to public policy in its various aspects. This we have done thoughtlessly without inquiring whether the burden can be effectively borne." (Allen, 1964, p. 4) It is important to realize that efforts to enforce borderline crime laws represent an immense cost to the agencies of crime control. While few laymen may be aware of it, only a relatively small proportion of police effort involves crimes against the person and serious property crime. For example, about a third of all arrests in the United States are for public drunkenness— an offense some would characterize as victimless, though it does not have the exchange feature focused on here. It has been estimated that the handling of such offenders (excluding treatment and prevention efforts) costs at least $100 million annually. (Morris and Hawkins, 1970, p. 6) According to

a recent report commissioned by the Ford Foundation, the
federal government spent in 1972 over $125 million on en-
forcement of drug control laws. (Goldberg and DeLong, 1972,
pp. 302–305) And a study of the laws against marijuana
estimated that (in 1968) California alone spent some $72
million in an effort to enforce that particular prohibition.
(Kaplan, 1971, p. 30) According to Packer, assuming an estimated total expenditure on law enforcement (nationally, in
1965) of around four and a half billion, "it may not be unreasonable to suppose that a hundred million dollars is a con-
servative estimate for gambling offenses. An extrapolation of
past trends suggests that this figure will double in ten years."
(Packer, 1968, p. 351)

It is because of their transactional nature—and the evidentiary difficulties such situations present—that crimes without victims are particularly costly to administer. Sociologist
Albert Reiss, who has done extensive research on patterns of
police work, very likely understates the point when he notes
that, "to make a case on the basis of evidence other than of-
ficer or citizen testimony involves considerably more effort
for the police than would be required if citizens generated the
complaint." (Reiss, 1971, p. 113) Lacking direct complainants, law enforcers become dependent for evidence on a variety of unsavory techniques—use of informers and decoys,
clandestine surveillance, wiretapping and other types of "bugging," surprise ("no-knock") raids, and the like. These methods, which are extremely time-consuming and hence expensive, are widely recognized to be an inevitable corollary of the
attempt to legally ban consensual (and often private) transactions.

According to a major study of narcotics enforcement techniques, "Without a network of informers—usually civilians, sometimes police—narcotics police cannot operate." (Skolnick, 1966, p. 120) Enforcement officials not only condone the use of stool pigeons (often euphemistically named "informants" or "special employees"), they actually pride themselves on the ability to develop such information networks and to manipulate the rewards necessary to sustain them. Apart from raising constitutional objections to such methods and voicing concern over the broad social implications of widespread police reliance on them, critics note that the informer system invariably implies indirect police support of addiction or criminality. Whatever the specific nature of the bargain, there is always "an implied understanding between the policeman and the informer that the policeman will protect the informer's criminal status." (Skolnick, 1966, p. 132) While perhaps few narcotics enforcers today directly provide drugs to addicts in exchange for information, it is common practice to pay the "expenses" of informants, which really amounts to the same thing. As another observer notes:

> The use of addict "stool pigeons" is so common that it is sometimes an embarrassment to the police. It tends to create a class of law violator who is to a degree and for varying periods of time exempt from the penalties of the law. Because of the secrecy shrouding the informer, the police sometimes arrest each other's stool pigeons and the latter sometimes try to make buys from each other. Arrested addicts sometimes indignantly ask to be released on the grounds that they are working for the police. (Lindesmith, 1967, p. 49)

Reliance on decoys (such as those who make the "buys" in which successful narcotics investigations culminate) is also central to the enforcement of anti-prostitution and anti-homo-sexuality laws. The common vice squad technique of luring streetwalkers into acts of solicitation has so little overall impact on prostitution and is so unpalatable that even enforcement officers hesitate to express approval of this method. In the police department Skolnick studied, all policemen interviewed claimed that surveillance accounted for most prostitution arrests whereas in fact (systematic data revealed) over half of such arrests stemmed from decoy activity. (Skolnick, 1966, pp. 100–103) However discreditable they may be, similar entrapment techniques have often been used to catch homosexuals. (*UCLA Law Review*, 1966, pp. 690–707) Although it is sometimes argued that decoys rarely elicit criminal acts that would not have occurred anyway, the legal line between legitimate investigation and entrapment (in which case the decoy is considered to have acted as an *agent provocateur*) is an extremely hazy one. That vice squad operatives may not be hesitant to take a chance on crossing this line is suggested by the following statement, based on careful research in Los Angeles County:

> . . . suggestive conduct by decoys may induce the situational offender to make a solicitation that otherwise would not have been made. Decoys have been reported to operate by standing outside of bars "licking their lips" and rubbing their bodies as customers exit the premises. One bar owner described overhearing a decoy tell a suspect that he had an erection and "wanted to be taken care of." Several decoys admitted to affecting the manner of a homosexual by "swishing" in bars and tapping their feet while using commodes in public restrooms. (*UCLA Law Review*, 1966, pp. 705–706)

The same study documents the extensive use of systematic (and often covert) surveillance—particularly of public restrooms, and not merely at beaches and parks but also in department stores, bus depots, gas stations, and other buildings open to the public—in attempts to get evidence of overt homosexual acts. As the researchers note, "If the police are unable to eliminate homosexual use of a location by patrolling, or by decoy enforcement, they may establish a hidden observation post in the location. The police then can observe the premises and, when an offense is committed, enter and make the arrest." (*UCLA Law Review*, 1966, p. 708) Complicated surveillance techniques are similarly required in efforts to develop adequate evidence against illegal abortionists. While initial leads sometimes are provided when an illegal abortion results in death or hospitalization, preparing a case for prosecution usually entails elaborate long-term surveillance and eventually some kind of surprise raid on the illegal practitioner's office. (Schur, 1965, pp. 35–38)

Attempts to enforce a legal ban on gambling also imply a reliance on questionable information-gathering procedures. Apart from so-called national security investigations, most officially-sanctioned wiretapping and other "bugging" occurs in connection with anti-gambling and anti-narcotics enforcement efforts. Indeed it is no exaggeration to say that the victimless crime area is dominated (and inevitably so) by all of the enforcement techniques that give rise to serious constitutional objection (on such grounds as compulsory self-incrimination, illegal search and seizure, and invasion of right to privacy). Characteristically, it was narcotics enforcement activity that led to several recent and much-publicized incidents in which plainclothesmen broke into private homes, destroying property and terrorizing the occupants—who, it turned out, happened to be completely innocent of involvement in drug offenses. (Wicker, 1973, p. 37)

If these methods were effective, perhaps one might justify them. Yet almost without exception disinterested observers, including law enforcement officials, have long recognized the patent unenforceability of the victimless crime laws. Despite the publicity given to occasional "crackdowns" on streetwalkers, drug sellers or dealers in pornography, to prosecutions of abortion "rings" or illicit gambling operations, and to raids on gay bars, there is little evidence of any appreciable success in curtailing the activities against which these laws are directed. The "revolving door" practice with respect to prostitution—in which streetwalkers are routinely hauled into court, fined, bailed out and back on the job in short order—typifies the aura of hypocrisy and futility that surrounds the attempt to enforce legislation against such borderline crimes:

> The actual situation in the city is that prostitution is accepted by everyone—police, judges, clerks, and lawyers. Arrest and prosecution are purely gestures that have to be made to keep up the facade of public morality. The method of dealing with it is simply a form of harassment, not a form of prevention, abolition, or punishment. There is no conviction at any level that prostitution is a crime on anyone's part, only a total and satisfied acceptance of the double standard, excusing the male, accusing the female. There is also a curious fascination with the prostitutes, "the girls," a geniality toward them, friendliness even, in the sense of familiarity. (Millett, *et al.*, 1973, p. 143)

Probably the only victimless crime in respect of which serious claims of enforcement effectiveness have been advanced
is the sale of narcotics. However, it has long been apparent
that police efforts in this area, while often falling heavily on
the user and small-time (usually addicted) pusher, have had
little impact in reducing the operations of the higher-ups in
what has become a well-organized distribution network. Most
observers (including its own research consultants) would
probably dispute the statement of the President's Crime Commission that, "There are persuasive reasons to believe that
enforcement of these laws has caused a significant reduction
in the flow of these drugs." (President's Commission, 1967b,
p. 8) Although specific enforcement drives may well have
short-term effects on the availability of drugs in particular
communities, there clearly have been no indications that such
efforts have overall significantly curbed the use of drugs. As a
recent exhaustive review of the evidence prepared for Consumers Union notes, "The only conclusion possible from either
the bureau [the federal Bureau of Narcotics and Dangerous
Drugs] estimate or the NIMH [National Institute of Mental
Health] estimate is that the decades of enforcement of the
Harrison Act and of countless other state and federal laws
designed to stamp out opiate addiction have been a losing
battle." (Brecher, *et al.*, 1972, p. 62) An early attempt to
assess the effects of New York's recently-revised drug laws
(which now provide extremely high mandatory minimum sen-
tences for most drug offenses other than mere possession of
small amounts of marijuana) found that, "the chief result of
the law was to drive drug dealing further underground, not to
dry it up." (Farber, 1973, p. 1) Some of the enormous costs

involved in such control efforts are suggested by the fact that administering the revised New York law has required the setting up of special courts and the appointment of new judges (an early estimate was that New York City alone would need 168 new courts and the same number of new judges to deal with the anticipated volume of drug arrests). (Ferretti, 1973, p. E3)

Anti-abortion laws have a similar record of failure. Very likely it is true that making abortion a crime deters some women from it. But for a great many years it has also been quite clear that the demand for the right to rid themselves of unwanted pregnancies—among women of all socio-economic strata, races, and religions—has been enormous. There is no evidence whatsoever that criminalizing this operation has appreciably reduced this demand or its satisfaction (by illegal means, when legal ones have been unavailable). (Lader, 1966, and Calderone, 1958)

In other victimless crime areas, the law's inability to curb much-desired transactions is again readily apparent. In the case of pornography, one might expect that concerted police action in a specific locale could largely erase from public view signs of the illicit traffic. Yet no reasonable enforcement spokesman would claim the ability to substantially curtail the willing exchange of pornographic materials. Likewise, there is not even an expressed intent to reduce homosexual acts underlying the harassing tactics involved in implementing anti-homosexuality statutes. And, as we have seen, much the same can be said of the enforcement activity directed at prostitution. Equally applicable to all of these areas is the following assessment of the attempt to ban gambling: "People have been arrested, prosecuted, and convicted, but the prohibited conduct has flourished. The law may operate in some measure to diminish demand, but it is clear that criminal enforcement does not begin to control the problem." (President's Commission, 1967a, p. 100)

Crimes without victims, in short, reflect or produce a policy of regulation or containment, rather than one that seriously aims at eliminating the proscribed behavior. Enforcement authorities are well aware not only of the practical obstacles to enforcing these laws but also of the relatively low level of public support for them. Under such circumstances—and given the continuing, albeit weakened, demand that they take some action in these areas—there is little alternative to falling back on sporadic and selective enforcement, petty harassment —in general, on practices that can at best shield the offending behavior from public view and proclaim a value commitment that most observers now recognize as being largely an empty one. As we shall see, these situations hold other consequences for police work; in particular, they open up widespread opportunities for corruption. But what is worth emphasizing here is that the police have understood, sometimes more clearly than the public, the unenforceability of these laws. To appreciate this point fully, we must consider the economics of banning consensual transactions, for the unenforceability of victimless crime laws is largely a matter of supply and demand.

ECONOMIC EFFECTS

As Herbert Packer has perceptively noted, "Regardless of what we think we are trying to do, when we make it illegal to traffic in commodities for which there is an inelastic demand,

the effect is to secure a kind of monopoly profit to the entre-
preneur who is willing to break the law." (Packer, 1968, p.
279, and also Rogers, 1973, pp. 75–103) The elaboration of
a black market based on such proscription has, without any
question, been a central feature of our narcotics and abortion
situations. In both instances, efforts to cut off supply have, in
the face of overwhelming demand, utterly failed to deter potential suppliers. On the contrary, criminalization—which by
raising the risks of illicit traffic, and to some extent limiting
supply, encourages price increases and hence higher illicit
profits—actually nurtures and strengthens black market operations. There is no reason to believe that such an illicit traffic
could succeed if it faced competition with legal provision of
the desired goods or services at cost. As the drug consultants
to the Ford Foundation emphasize: "The illegality of heroin
is, of course, the sole reason for its high cost in this country.
In England, the pharmacy cost of heroin is $.04 per grain
(60 mg.), or $.00067 per mg. In the United States, the recent
street price is $30–$90 per grain, or $.50–$1.50 per mg.,
depending on the time and place of sale and the quantity and
quality of the drug." (Wald and Hutt, 1972, p. 28) Likewise,
the cost of abortion—which under routine hospital (or even
office) procedures need not be an expensive operation—has
escalated substantially under conditions of criminalization.

Claims that the demand in such instances is not necessarily
as compelling as was once believed (this has been asserted,
for example, by some students of the heroin situation), (Wilson, Moore, and Wheat, 1972) are not very persuasive. The
comment by Packer, that abortions are sought for "reasons of
overwhelming compulsion" (Packer, 1968, p. 344), is equally
germane to the heroin addict's demand for drugs. If demand

were in fact relatively elastic, it would not provide sufficient incentive for illicit trafficking in the face of militant enforcement efforts; yet the evidence from years of attempting to curb heroin (for example) indicates that this is not the case. The recent Consumers Union report comments:

> On rare occasions, it is true, the seizure of a very large shipment of heroin does cause a temporary shortage of black-market supplies within the United States. This, however, is hardly an objectionable event for the American distributors; on the contrary, it enables them to raise their prices even higher. Indeed, the profitability of the entire narcotics black market depends on untiring efforts of the law-enforcement agencies to hold the available supply down to the level of effective demand. (Brecher, *et al.*, 1972, p. 94)

In fact, the demand is so overwhelming that any degree of success in curtailing one means of supply simply gives rise to another. What one invariably finds, in the victimless crime situations, is an endless cycle (and competitive development) of techniques of law violation and law enforcement. Enforcers become adept at combatting a particular mode of drug smuggling, and a new more effective smuggling technique is adopted. The authorities' information networks are successful in disclosing professional gamblers, abortionists, or dealers in pornography, and illegal operatives in turn develop improved methods of concealment. Thus, even under optimal enforcement (and leaving aside for the moment the possibility of ensuring "protection" through the corruption of the enforcers), because high profits make it worth running high risks new ways of making available the much-desired supplies are always found.

Given this, it is hardly surprising that crimes without victims offer major opportunities for organized crime. Organized criminal groups, the President's Crime Commission noted, "participate in any illegal activity that offers maximum profit at minimum risk of law-enforcement interference. They offer goods and services that millions of Americans desire even though declared illegal by their legislature." (President's Commission, 1967c, p. 2) It is generally recognized that illegal gambling, which is highly organized, provides the largest sources of revenue for organized crime. As Packer points out:

> The combination of illegality and the need for organization produces a classic operation of the crime tariff. These monopoly profits then become available to sustain the activities of the criminal organization on a wide variety of fronts, including the penetration of legitimate and quasi-legitimate economic markets. There is some evidence that gambling profits are reinvested in the loan shark business, which is said to be the second largest source of revenue for organized crime. In a neat reverse twist, this business may then be used to place small-time independent bookmakers under financial obligation and thus to coerce them into becoming part of a syndicated gambling operation, with resulting increases in the profits of the organization. (Packer, 1968, p. 350)

Another disturbing economic aspect of victimless crime situations involves systematic socio-economic differentials in access to the desired goods or services and in enforcement of the law. When one makes criminal the sale of these goods or services, it typically follows (to an extent that would not have to pertain under legal market conditions) that the quality of what is supplied and the safety under which this occurs vary enormously depending upon the buyer's purchasing power. Again this has been most dramatically evident with respect to abortion and narcotics—although it seems also true, in varying degrees, of prostitution, illegal gambling, and the traffic in pornography. When abortion has been against the law, the sophisticated woman of means often has had relatively easy access to physicians or other skilled operatives, or she may even manage to obtain a "therapeutic" hospital abortion. (Though even for the affluent, the search for a competent abortionist can be long and complicated. See Lee, 1969.) The not so affluent abortion-seeker usually has been able to afford only the services of less well-trained and careful practitioners (thus running serious risk of injury), or she has been forced (at still greater danger to herself) to attempt a self-induced termination of pregnancy.

Similarly, in the case of drug addiction the addict's overall situation is significantly determined by his financial position. The well-to-do addict (which includes the doctor-addict, who often can maintain his own drug supply from legal sources) frequently can support his habit without financial difficulty and in a relatively safe manner. In contrast the addict of limited means almost invariably faces an intolerable financial burden and more likely than not is driven to money-producing crime (see below) to obtain the funds to buy illicit drugs. Law enforcement practices reflect such differentials, and at the same time exacerbate them. The police realize the impossibility of full enforcement, and so feel a need to set priorities that will guide their efforts in the victimless crime area. They tend to concentrate on those activities that have the highest public visibility, that seem most directly related to serious crime, and with respect to which they will receive the strongest support from the other agencies of criminal justice and from the general public. The ghetto drug-user, who (necessarily) is enmeshed in underworld-linked distribution mechanisms and most likely is pushing drugs and/or committing other crimes to support his habit, is an easier enforcement target than less visible addicts or remote (usually non-addicted) distributors.

Likewise it is clear that anti-prostitution efforts concentrate on lower-class streetwalkers rather than the more hidden and affluent call-girls; and that gambling enforcement focuses on the poor man's "numbers" racket rather than the rich man's wagering activities. (A panel of prominent lawyers recently recommended legalization of the numbers game, stressing the inequities that exist when off-track betting is legalized but no lower-class equivalent, or one meaningful to blacks, is legitimated.) (Delaney, 1973, p. 11, and Geis, 1973, pp. 179–180) Undoubtedly some similar differentials exist in efforts to enforce the laws against sale of pornography and against homosexual behavior (in the latter case primarily as regards homosexual prostitution, but also perhaps with reference to harassment of bars, clubs, and other facilities). As one might expect and as at least the drug use and numbers game examples imply, selective enforcement along economic lines often amounts to racially selective enforcement as well.

When one considers this together with the social conditions and discrimination that disproportionately drive blacks into some of these proscribed behaviors (at least drug use and prostitution), one has to recognize that a pattern of multiple discrimination exists here. Further, sexual, as well as racial, discrimination is present in prostitution, of which one commentator asserts: "Prostitution is really the only crime in the penal law where two people are doing a thing mutually agreed upon and yet only one, the female partner, is subjected to arrest." (Millett *et al.*, 1973, p. 146) As the same writer goes on to note, a recent New York provision making the male client (the "John") also guilty of an offense, is simply not enforced.

CREATING CRIMINALS

Crime laws, by definition, create criminals. This perspective has, unfortunately, been much neglected by many sociologists and psychologists researching and theorizing about the "causes" of crime. Preoccupied with the root causes of individual criminality (whether these be seen as lying in personality disposition or in socio-economic conditions), such researchers often have failed to consider how the impact of the law itself affects social behavior and outlooks. When attention has been paid to this matter, it has sometimes been assumed (in a way that now appears unwarranted) that most of the law's effects will be socially desirable. Actually one of the major consequences of criminalizing mutually desired exchanges is the creation of much additional crime (that would not exist if the consensual behavior were legal) and the proliferation of criminal self-conceptions among the "offending" individuals.

To begin with, victimless crimes as we have seen open up a wide range of criminal occupations. Professional drug traffickers and illicit gambling operators, pornography dealers, illegal abortionists, pimps and others (besides the prostitutes themselves) who profit illegally from prostitution (both heterosexual and homosexual), all owe their existence to these attempts to ban consensual transactions. This is largely true as well of those engaged in blackmailing homosexuals—for even if homosexuality would be socially discreditable in the absence of criminalization, the homosexual's vulnerability is greatly heightened when he is subject to criminal prosecution. There is, furthermore, little doubt that in the United States substantial proportions of property crime and prostitution are directly attributable to the efforts of drug addicts to support their habit. Debate continues regarding the precise relation between addiction and crime, but there is now overwhelming agreement on at least the following points: addicts tend to engage in money-producing rather than violent crimes; and regardless of what they might have done had they not been addicted (or what they did before), once fully dependent on opiates most American addicts *must* turn to illegal acts if they are to purchase the drugs they need. Although a few commentators continue to insist that legal availability of drugs would have little effect in reducing rates of property crime (Wilson, *et al.,* 1972), this is distinctly a minority view.

One recent assessment—based on an estimate of 250,000 addicts nationally, and an average cost per day per addict of $30—concluded that funds obtained by addicts through property crime may well total annually $653,441,250, at a cost to the victims of $1,698,947,250, and that another $326,720,-625 is obtained through prostitution. (Holahan, 1972, pp. 292–293) The experience of Great Britain, where traditionally addiction has been treated as a medical problem and the addict has been able to obtain drugs legally by prescription (and at practically no cost under the National Health Service) is also instructive on this point. (Lindesmith, 1967) In recent years this policy has not prevented some increase in the number of addicts—an increase that has caused authorities there to tighten the procedures for such prescribing, even though the dimensions of the addiction problem remain modest by American standards. Yet, as recent authoritative accounts make clear, no significant amount of addict-crime (and no substantial illicit traffic in opiates) has emerged under the British approach. (See Scull, 1972, pp. 282–314, and May, 1972, pp. 345–394.) Considering all available evidence, it is difficult not to conclude that criminalization of opiate use in the United States has greatly amplified our overall crime problem.

The addiction situation reveals to an unusual extent the possible development of a criminalization-criminality cycle. When access to legal sources is barred, and as the addict increasingly is treated as an enemy of society, he almost necessarily becomes one. Forced into criminal acts, immersed in underworld-related supply networks, and ever conscious of the need to evade the police, his outlooks as well as behavior become more and more anti-social. Should he experience actual criminal conviction and incarceration (either in a prison, or else under one of the recent schemes of enforced "treatment"), the cycle is pushed one step further and, most likely, the negative consequences will be intensified. (Although several voluntary drug treatment programs claim considerable success, the results of most compulsory efforts have been far from impressive.) In varying degrees, all victimless crime situations produce some unnecessary and undesirable criminalization of individuals. Even where statutes can only be enforced sporadically and haphazardly, the individual "offender" may still run considerable risk of direct encounter with the law. Thus a knowledgeable observer of the homosexual community has recently noted that, "the average homosexual has ample cause to fear arrest. My conversations and interviews with hundreds of gay men during seven years of research show that nearly all of those over 30, and approximately half of the men under that age, have been questioned or charged by law enforcement officials in connection with their sexual activities." (Humphreys, 1972, p. 19, and *UCLA Law Review*, 1966) Reporting on another grossly underenforced law, Kaplan states that despite the relatively low proportion of all users that are legally proceeded against, "In California during 1968 approximately one-fourth of all felony complaints were for violation of the marijuana laws. More than 34,000 adults and 17,000 juveniles were arrested for marijuana offenses." (Kaplan, 1971, p. 30)

Where abortion has been illegal, the woman submitting to the operation usually has been technically liable to prosecution, as well as the person performing it. Even though such provisions ordinarily have gone unenforced, knowledge of her criminal status (while seeming to have little deterrent effect) may have a harsh psychological impact on the abortion-seeker. Experience in other countries that have broadly permitted legal termination of pregnancy (and more recently in American jurisdictions that similarly have done so) make clear that ordinarily there need be no great risk of psychological complications following a routine hospital abortion. But where the operation is not permitted legally, and even if the woman is unaware that she herself is technically liable under the law, the secrecy and sordid conditions surrounding most illegal operations—along with the likelihood of physical pain and serious medical risk—are almost certain to produce or exacerbate feelings of guilt and remorse. If the prospect of such an experience were in fact to deter many women from ending pregnancies, then perhaps it might be argued (at least by those who believe abortion is always undesirable or immoral) that the production of such feelings is justifiable. As already noted, however, the overwhelming weight of available evidence indicates that this is not the case.

The social and psychological ramifications of criminalization are much more significant, of course, when the legal proscription covers not simply a single incident of law violation (as an abortion usually is, in the life of the woman who obtains one), but instead activity that represents an important and continuing aspect of the total life pattern of the individual involved. As we have just seen, some of the most deleterious of these long-term consequences are readily apparent in the relation between the illegality of addictive drugs and crime. But being pushed into overt criminal acts is only one example of the continuing degradation of persons subject to victimless crime laws. The constant need to practice concealment, a special vulnerability to exploitation, and a frequent encountering of serious social discrimination, are typical features of these situations. Recent sociological interest in "labeling" processes has increased our awareness of the part played by negative social reactions in stigmatizing deviating individuals and in propelling (rather than inhibiting) the development of deviant careers and self-conceptions. (see Schur, 1971; Becker, 1963; Erikson, 1962; Kitsuse, 1962) When a significant aspect of one's life behavior is proscribed by law, these discrediting processes are almost bound to be intensified.

The self-hatred and tendency toward self-segregation that have often been cited as being prevalent among homosexuals illustrate the difficulties involved in coming to grips with a socially (and legally) discreditable identity. As one writer (who feels he has achieved personal liberation through self-affirmation as homosexual) comments, "even now there are times when I flinch from being identified as a homosexual, for one feels the contempt that the identification brings. It requires a self-assurance that very few, either gay or straight, possess, to be fully immune to the effect of social disapproval." (Altman, 1973, p. 64) The occupational distribution of homosexuals has long been recognized as being heavily influenced by the need for concealment. On the one hand, there is a variety of stereotypical "homosexual jobs" (hairdresser, designer, various other work in the arts) where disclosure need not jeopardize occupational security. In other areas of work, the difficulty of maintaining high-level positions if one openly acknowledges one's homosexuality is pronounced. Humphreys notes that, "a disproportionately high number of male homosexuals find employment as hospital orderlies and technicians, travelling salesmen, retail sales clerks, short order cooks, and waiters. I doubt that gay men gravitate to these jobs because they enjoy changing bed linen, washing dishes, waiting tables, or stocking merchandise. The greater probability is that these are the only positions open to discreditable individuals." (Humphreys, 1972, p. 34)

Recently, when a former New York City Health Services Administrator, Howard J. Brown, publicly acknowledged his homosexuality, he noted that while his life's ambition had been to be a small-town doctor, he came to New York to avoid the problems that would have confronted him in establishing such a practice in a Middle-Western community. Fear of losing your job and reputation, he stated, "pervade everything you do." (Chambers, 1973, pp. 1, 42) Evidence from situations where consenting private homosexual acts have been decriminalized (for example, in England and also in the State of Illinois) makes clear that removal of the legal ban will hardly eliminate either social disapproval or the considerable discomfort the homosexual consequently experiences. Nonetheless, the knowledge that one's basic sexual orientation makes one a "criminal," together with the ever-present concern to avoid detection and prosecution, must greatly increase these pressures and strains. At least some of the elaboration of a separate "gay community" (which, at times, involves economic exploitation by unscrupulous or even underworld-related businessmen) is also attributable to these pressures. As Altman points out, "Most homosexuals, given a fully accepting society, would, I suspect, eschew constant gay company; one has interests that extend beyond sexual orientation." (Altman, 1973, p. 64)

Sociologists have recently emphasized that imputations of deviance take on a kind of all-encompassing quality. Once we identify an individual as deviant, we tend to see him or her only and totally in that light. This process of "status degradation" (Garfinkel, 1956, pp. 420–424; Goffman, 1961; Kitsuse, 1962; Becker, 1963) and identity-reconstruction becomes especially pronounced when the socially discreditable behavior or condition is also against the law. Many of the problems faced by homosexuals, such as those just mentioned (and also the degrading and highly questionable restrictions placed on their employment—in such areas as teaching, the military, and the civil service) stem from the tendency to label such individuals in this far-reaching manner. The difficulties ex-addicts experience obtaining jobs, and the tarnished reputation that former prostitutes seem unable to shed, similarly reflect these tenacious degradation processes. As an ex-prostitute has succinctly remarked, "I don't feel that I'm a whore now, but the social stigma attached to prostitution is a very powerful thing. It makes a kind of total state out of prostitution so that the whore is always a whore. It's as if—you did it once, you become it." (Millett et al., 1973, p. 65) Increasingly specialists and policymakers are coming to believe that this sort of total long-term banishment from "respectable" society (which is at least abetted by criminalization) causes a hardship that cannot be justified. Calling for a reassessment of policies and practices relating to employment of homosexuals, the National Institute of Mental Health Task Force on Homosexuality asserted:

> Present employment policies generally deal with the homosexual individual as if homosexuality were a specific and homogeneous category of behavior, and tend to ignore the wide range of variation that exists. We recognize that some homosexuals, like some heterosexuals, may be unsuitable employees in some situations because they do not exercise reasonable control over their sexual tendencies or activities.
>   Second, in highly sensitive positions, the possibility that a homosexual may be subject to blackmail or undue influence may affect the suitability of a homosexual individual for such employment, although changes in our present laws concerning homosexuality may ultimately eliminate this. (NIMH Task Force, 1972, pg. 6)

CORRUPTION AND DISRESPECT FOR LAW

Most careful observers now acknowledge that crimes without victims provide an unparalleled invitation to police corruption. Such corruption has two main sources: the enormous discretion vested in the police when full enforcement is recognized to be impossible; and the existence of highly ambivalent public opinion with respect to the substance of these laws. Packer notes that the trouble with police discretion is "simply that it is lawless, in the literal sense of that term." (Packer, 1968, p. 290) We have already considered various abuses of due process that become prevalent in the absence of complainant-generated evidence, and also the discriminatory enforcement patterns that may emerge due to the inevitably selective nature of legal action under such conditions. Since the police have extremely broad discretion in deciding whether to proceed or not to proceed against a potential "offender," victimless crime laws set the stage for bribery as well.

Illegal gambling provides the strongest illustration of such corruption. According to the Knapp Commission on police corruption in New York City, "The collection of tribute by police from gamblers has traditionally been extremely well organized and has persisted in virtually unchanged form for years despite periodic scandals, departmental reorganizations, massive transfers in and out of the units involved, and the folding of some gambling operations and the establishment of new ones." (*Knapp Commission Report,* 1972, p. 71) As the Commission went on to note:

> Police officers, sharing the general attitude that gambling does no harm, themselves regard gambling money as "clean" graft. But, despite the changed attitudes toward gambling, most forms of gambling remain illegal, and corrupt policemen at the time of the investigations considered gamblers fair game.
>
> As for gamblers, they were found to regard payments to the police as a necessary business expense. They often pointed out that a numbers operation couldn't exist unless

it was under police auspices. As one gambler told the Commission, the police "are the insurance company, and unless
you pay your monthly rent, you can't operate." (*Knapp
Commission Report,* 1972, p. 73)

The Knapp Commission, and other investigators, have found
similar corruption to be extremely prevalent in other victimless
crime areas. The above comment regarding "insurance" is
equally applicable to the illegal abortion situation; indeed, except where the entire proscribed transaction can take place
under conditions of complete privacy (which is usually unlikely) no type of illicit supplier can operate for long without
police complicity. Payoffs to the police are known to occur
frequently in connection with narcotics dealing, and the main-
tenance of premises for purposes of prostitution. Similarly
police "shakedown" of homosexuals is a common practice.
Likewise, the Knapp Commission found that illegal after-hour
clubs catering to homosexuals operated openly and without
interference despite their illegal status:

> The Commission found that many of these unlicensed bars
> made payoffs to division plainsclothesmen and detectives
> who were charged with enforcing laws against them, to insure
> that the bars would be allowed to operate virtually unhin-
> dered by police action. The payments were substantial, rang-
> ing up to $2,000 a month for the largest and most lucrative
> club. The understanding between bar owners and police was
> that occasional token arrests would be made to keep up a
> facade of police alertness, but that the arrests would be han-
> dled in such a manner that they did not seriously disrupt
> business. Arrests were generally limited to a handful of minor
> employees, and were made quietly, so that customers were
> not harassed or intimidated. Seizure of liquor generally con-

sisted of police taking two or three half-empty bottles for evidence and leaving the main supply intact. (*Knapp Commission Report*, 1972, pp. 140–141)

Among its recommendations for reducing police corruption, the Commission proposed severely limiting police responsibility for enforcement of regulations concerning such establishments; it also recommended complete abolition of the laws against gambling, and "increased study and attention . . . to ways other than criminal sanctions for dealing with the addict." (*Knapp Commission Report*, 1972, pp. 18–19)

One can indeed argue, on several grounds, that the victimless crime laws represent a substantial threat to the overall integrity of the American legal system. All of the negative consequences of criminalization that we have examined serve to make these particular prohibitions disreputable. But beyond that, several of them encourage a general cynicism toward the law that may influence public conceptions of the entire system of criminal justice. In the first place, many will feel there is a strong element of hypocrisy involved in maintaining on the lawbooks provisions that are so blatantly unenforceable. This reaction is likely to be reinforced when large numbers of people view a particular ban as being unnecessary or undesirable, quite apart from whether or not it could be enforced. Both Packer and Kaplan note, for example, the widespread conviction that marijuana is a relatively harmless drug, and argue that given this belief continued criminalization will contribute to what the former terms the "particularly severe crisis of confidence on the part of youth toward the society in which they live." (Packer, 1968, p. 340; Kaplan, 1971, pp. 33–37; see also, National Commission on Marihuana and Drug Abuse, 1972.)

The patterns of selective enforcement and police corruption invariably found in victimless crime situations further undermine respect for the law. As noted above, such tendencies are at least in part attributable to the large element of police discretion in these areas. A study group of the American Friends Service Committee has stated that, "Discretion serves only to blunt or twist the principles of justice and legality, for these are dependent upon the uniform application of general rules." (A.F.S.C., 1971) Yet where the law seeks to curb widely desired consensual exchanges such uniform application becomes virtually impossible. We have seen, furthermore, that the uneven impact of actual enforcement measures tends to mirror and reinforce more general patterns of discrimination (along socioeconomic, racial and ethnic, sexual, and perhaps generational lines) within the society. As a consequence, such enforcement (ineffective as it may be in producing conformity) almost certainly reinforces feelings of alienation already prevalent within major segments of the population.

When recognition of discriminatory enforcement is accompanied by an experiencing of corruption as an ordinary element, one can anticipate cynicism and alienation in the highest degree. According to the Knapp Commission:

> Youngsters raised in New York ghettos, where gambling abounds, regard the law as a joke when all their lives they have seen police officers coming and going from gambling establishments and taking payments from gamblers. Many ghetto people who have grown up watching police performance in relation to gambling and narcotics are absolutely convinced that all policemen are getting rich on their share of the profits of these two illegal activities . . . (*Knapp Commission Report,* 1972, p. 90)

Although there are those who would argue that any recent decline in respect for the law is attributable to "permissiveness" and inadequate training, many other observers would insist that a legal system gets the respect it deserves. Here again, one should emphasize that the citizenry's appraisals of justice will most likely be shaped by observations of (or knowledge or beliefs about) the actual workings of the legal apparatus, rather than simply reflecting approval or disapproval of the formal provisions on the statute books. The branding of large segments of our population as "criminal" that we have been considering is, as we have seen, not just a symbolic act. It has very real consequences for the individuals involved, many of whom even in the absence of such criminalization would be likely to have strong grievances against the society in which they live. In a recent analysis of victimless crime laws, Gilbert Geis has commented "To the extent that a society thrusts from its core nonconformists and then takes harsh measures to repress them, it will create a resistant force in its midst." (Geis, 1970, pp. 260–261) This may well prove to have been one of the major unintended consequences of such legislation.

III
THE CHANGING CONTEXT

POLITICIZING DEVIANCE

Recent sociological studies have highlighted the element of group conflict that often underlies deviance and the social re-

action to it. Indeed, one writer goes so far as to assert that,
"Deviance is the name of the conflict game in which individuals or loosely organized small groups with little power are
strongly feared by a well-organized, sizable minority or majority who have a large amount of power." (Lofland, 1969, p.
14) Of course the tendency to view rule-violation in individualistic terms, to assume it can be fully explained by reference
to the alleged special characteristics of "offenders," is deeply
engrained in our society. Even among those sociologists who
now stress the effects of societal reaction on the deviating individual, there may sometimes be a failure to consider the
broader context of conflicting group interests. Yet one cannot
have violations without rules, and it seems clear that usually
the making and applying of rules (including legal rules) will
uphold certain systems of values and collective interests to the
detriment, if not the exclusion, of others. In a culturally pluralistic society such as ours, in which there is far from a complete consensus concerning social value priorities, this is un-
deniably the case.

Of crucial significance for the debate about crimes without
victims is the tendency of individuals subject to such laws increasingly to view their situations in this light. Rather than
accepting the previously prevailing definitions of their behavior, such persons are beginning to actively resist what they see
as nothing more than the imposition upon them of other people's rules. Thus we now find occurring on quite a large scale
what has been termed the "politicization of deviance." (Horowitz and Liebowitz, 1968, p. 282) Individuals who once were
widely viewed as offenders are developing a heightened awareness of their collective interests, as a result of which they are
organizing to further shared goals through political action.

Perhaps the most dramatic illustration of this is the gay liberation movement. Whereas so-called homophile organizations have existed in the United States for a good many years, until recently they tended to emphasize social and self-help functions and to maintain a moderate and rather defensive posture. In the five years since its inception, the more militant gay movement (which is usually said to have come into being during the summer of 1969, through an incident in New York involving active confrontation between homosexuals and the police) has grown rapidly. There has been a proliferation of militant organizations that take as their goal complete "liberation" of homosexuals rather than mere "acceptance." (Humphreys, 1972; Altman, 1973) Indeed, various of these groups frequently appear to be vying with one another to demonstrate the highest degree and most effective forms of militancy. Yet, despite the dilution in solidarity that this factionalism may suggest, the collective impact of their efforts may already have been substantial. These organizations have, among other things, lobbied for the repeal of anti-homosexual laws, organized public demonstrations in support of homosexual rights, publicized the opinions and votes of political candidates on homosexuality-related issues, sponsored political candidates of their own, urged bloc voting by homosexuals, and challenged anti-homosexual discrimination by supporting test cases in the courts. According to some commentators, one of the most significant results of such activity has been the development or reinforcement of "gay pride" among homosexuals themselves. A new sense of identity, both individually and collectively, is making it less and less likely that homosexuals will acquiesce in their own social and legal oppression.

Another major example of politicization—perhaps even

more striking in terms of apparent short-term success—has been the action of the women's movement in seeking to overturn anti-abortion laws. (Lader, 1973) Here again, a potential impetus to change existed earlier in the experience of women who had undergone illegal abortions, together with the more systematic critique of repressive abortion laws developed by medical, legal, and sociological specialists. Yet in the absence of a well-developed collective consciousness among abortion-seekers and women generally, the most that could realistically be anticipated in this area was a patently unsatisfactory piece-meal reform. With the advent of the recent women's movement, and the public proclamation of abortion as a major women's issue, rapid and quite thoroughgoing legal change became a real possibility. Notwithstanding the gradual development over the years of changes in public attitudes toward abortion and the laws against it, there is good reason to believe that collective action organized through the women's movement played the pivotal role in producing the recent dramatic steps toward its de-criminalization. (The occasional setbacks —as when lobbying by Right-to-Life groups led to repeal of radical legislation in New York, which was then maintained only through direct gubernatorial action—in no way belie this interpretation. On the contrary, such events again underscore the general politicization of the abortion issue.)

Both of these movements, as well as that for the de-criminalization of marijuana use (which also has achieved considerable success), reflect broader currents of socio-cultural change in American society. Undoubtedly, experience with the earlier civil rights and anti-war movements helped to provide models for militant efforts to achieve social change, and to some extent encouragement in pursuing such efforts. The general develop-

ment among youth of a so-called counterculture has also provided considerable support for efforts to break down various
patterns of enforced conformity. On at least some issues, the
gay liberation movement, the women's movement, and the
youth movement appear to intersect in such a way as to
strengthen each other. Repudiation of sham and hypocrisy, and
preparedness to re-evaluate even long-held moral beliefs—both
central features of the contemporary counterculture—have
further encouraged the reassessment of victimless crime situations. And as noted earlier, the influence of scientific studies in
demolishing stereotypes and disseminating accurate information about these situations has been considerable.

Along with such developments (and particularly reflecting
the new militancy of erstwhile deviants), there has been increased public exposure to the personal outlooks and reactions
of individuals who have directly experienced the impact of
these laws. Such statements convey a reality and immediacy
that often is lacking in sociological and legal critiques. They
tend, furthermore, to highlight the inadequacy of efforts to
analyze these issues in an abstract totally non-empirical way.
These people (and the organized movements which they increasingly comprise) are asserting, in effect, that they reject
such an approach; they are demanding attention to the facts.
That this insistence has a special authority behind it may be
implicit in Kate Millett's recent comment regarding decriminalization of prostitution: "It will be the prostitutes themselves,
the persons involved and informed, who are best qualified to
direct the decisions and strategy of such a campaign and its
targets: the vice squad, city hall, the legislature." (Millett *et
al.,* 1973, p. 109)

THE SEARCH FOR ALTERNATIVES

One commonplace assumption being challenged through the politicization of victimless crime situations is that the proscribed behaviors necessarily constitute social problems. It is the proposed "solution," many now assert, that is the gist of the "problem," rather than the behavior that elicited such control efforts in the first place. If one accepts the view that the dominant social and legal norms emerge out of conflicts or contests between competing interests and values, then it would seem to follow that the very meaning of the term "problem" is similarly problematic. Leaving aside the hypothetical case in which a set of identifiable conditions threatens the very survival of a society, there is no such thing as a scientifically ascertainable or demonstrable social problem. Rather, social problems are simply conditions about which influential segments of the society believe "something ought to be done." And the strength of these sentiments, it should be stressed, may vary according to time and to place.

The evidence cited above may be sufficient to convince many observers that indeed the consensual transactions in question would not represent serious problems for a society in the absence of the kind of reaction we have manifested toward them. However, we need not reach such a conclusion in order to sustain the case for de-criminalization. Even if one were to conclude that these behaviors (either all of them or some of them) should be considered problematic or disturbing in their own right, a determination that they are rendered more so under present policies than would be the case under alternative policies would seem to warrant a preference for de-criminaliza-tion. Making such an assessment is, of course, not an easy matter. Value judgments intrude at several stages of such a process (with respect to evaluating and weighing the relative importance of both means and ends). Yet, presumably one would only be justified in avoiding this effort if one were both to assert a system of *absolute* moral values relevant to these behaviors *and* to consider morally irrelevant the question of whether the assertion of such values really influences human behavior.

When confronted with the demand to consider policy alter-natives Americans often look for an easy way out. Susceptible to humanitarian appeals, they have been particularly likely to attempt to develop medical schemes that might serve as sub-stitutes for unworkable law enforcement approaches. Thus it has been argued that drug addiction should not be considered a crime because it is really a disease; likewise, that homosexu-als are disturbed individuals who should be helped by psychi-atry rather than hounded by the police. The fact that abortion is, after all, a standard medical procedure has very likely con-tributed to the relative acceptability of its de-criminalization. By the same token, the difficulty of conceiving of prostitution being conducted under medical auspices may impede change in that area (although if this reasoning is correct, then concern for limiting the spread of venereal disease could be a significant factor in support of arguments for revision of anti-prostitution laws).

There is now considerable recognition that, however pro-gressive they may seem at first glance, these efforts to define problematic situations in medical terms are far from being universally successful. As the trend toward politicization pro-

ceeds, the individuals involved become increasingly unwilling
to accept medical definitions of their behavior; the gay liberation movement's repudiation of the concept that homosexuality
is a disease or even "abnormal" is a striking case in point.
Similarly, large-scale service programs that leave the individual
subject to substantial medical control (such as enforced "civil
commitment" of addicts for treatment, or the granting of "therapeutic abortions" on approval by hospital medical boards)
have been found to be inadequate modifications of what has
remained a basically punitive policy.

The range of possible alternatives to current policies regarding the various behaviors considered in this essay is substantial,
and the issues pertaining to them are complex and variable.
The problems posed by state-organized gambling are different
from those presented by licensed prostitution; those involved
in a scheme for government regulation of marijuana distribution undoubtedly differ from those present in programs of
methadone or heroin-maintenance for opiate addicts. It is not
possible to include in this brief discussion detailed consideration of the pros and cons of such specific policy options. Yet
the question of alternative policies suggests several general
points that often have been obscured and that require at least
brief comment here. The first concerns the frequently implied
necessity of specifying a precise alternative.

Such necessity is not at all self-evident. As Packer has suggested, "The real alternative in many cases will turn out to be
doing nothing (as a matter of legal compulsion), or at any rate
doing less. Distasteful as that alternative may sometimes seem,
we need to press the inquiry whether it is not preferable to
doing what we are now doing." (Packer, 1968, p. 366) No-

body would argue that de-criminalization is a panacea. Experience in jurisdictions that have legislated one or another victimless crime out of existence makes it quite clear that such a step does not completely and smoothly eliminate perceived social problems overnight. Legal proscription is so intimately related to more general patterns of social disapproval that certain potential effects of de-criminalization can only be determined through long-term comparative analysis. Other short-term effects (including possible lessening of secondary harms) may be more readily apparent. However, we have virtually no evidence at all to support the claims one sometimes encounters to the effect that dire consequences are bound to follow de-criminalization. Typically, of course, such claims do involve long-term projections. Yet, as Geis recently noted, all too often there has been "the implicit assumption that failure to continue existing proscription of morally condemned behavior is apt to produce *only* untoward results. Actually, the results are apt to be of many different kinds, and a true measure of their totality almost an impossible task." (Geis, 1972, p. 8)

These comments may suggest a further point—one that is of particular significance. In our discussion so far, no explicit effort has been made to specify where the burden of argument and evidence ought to lie regarding the substance of the criminal law. As we have seen, there may be a strong case for believing that the provisions considered here do more harm than good. But there is a very substantial school of opinion asserting that—given the dangers of restricting personal liberty, and taking into account the potential for abuse—one should insist always on adequate justification of *recourse* to criminal proscription. If one adopts this view, then presumably it is the proponents of criminalization who must initially make their case: they must demonstrate that these provisions do more good than harm. This they most certainly have not done.

CONCLUSION

As we have seen, the argument against proscribing these consensual transactions does not stand or fall upon a demonstration that nobody is directly harmed by the activities in question. We have, however, insisted that to ignore the compelling social demand for these transactions—and the consequences that appear to flow directly from that demand—is to blind oneself to reality. To be sure, there may be instances (as in the areas of corporate crime and espionage, for example) where one might consider the criminalizing of consensual transactions to be warranted. In such cases, however, there is no reason to anticipate massive social harm resulting from criminalization. Furthermore, these may be among the offending behaviors that are most likely to be deterred by criminal sanctions. Available evidence indicates that the kinds of behavior we have been considering here are most unlikely to be significantly deterred through such measures. (For a good general discussion of deterrence see Zimring, 1971.)

To marshall empirical evidence as has been done here is not to argue for an extreme utilitarianism in which it is assumed that some kind of quantitative calculation can produce authoritative answers to complex moral questions. In the absence of universal moral consensus, assessments of evidence and weighings of alternatives will necessarily entail reference to particular value hierarchies; the reasoning by which an analyst would support his judgment can, of course, be made known and in turn be assessed by others. Inevitably a utilitarian or relativistic stance implies uncertainty. One who adopts such a stance denies himself as well as others the comfort of absolutes. Yet such uncertainty may not be inappropriate to a world in which presumably less-than-perfect policy decisions are made continuously, many of which have serious and at times predictable consequences for large numbers of people.

If we cannot have certainty in our recourse to the criminal law, perhaps at least we would be wise to exercise restraint. There appears to be good reason for believing that often the unintended consequences of criminalizing take on a greater significance than the intended ones. With this in mind, there is strong argument for adopting a minimal model of the appropriate use of the criminal justice system. The American Friends Service Committee study group recently concluded that reliance on the criminal law could only be justified if:

1. there is compelling social need to require compliance with a particular norm;

2. the law and its administration can be applied equally, so that all are weighed with the same scales and so that the human costs of enforcement are spread among the largest feasible number of offenders;

3. there is no less costly method of obtaining compliance; and

4. there is some substantial basis for assuming that the imposition of punishment will produce greater benefit for society than simply doing nothing. (A.F.S.C., 1971, p. 66)

48 *Edwin M. Schur*

By these criteria, the laws establishing crimes without victims are clearly lacking in justification.

REFERENCES

ALLEN, FRANCIS A., 1964. *The Borderland of Criminal Justice*. Chicago: University of Chicago Press.

ALTMAN, DENNIS, 1973. *Homosexual: Oppression and Liberation*. New York: Avon Books.

AMERICAN FRIENDS SERVICE COMMITTEE, 1971. *Struggle For Justice: A Report on Crime and Punishment in America*. New York: Hill and Wang.

BECKER, HOWARD S., 1963. *Outsiders*. New York: Free Press.

BRECHER, EDWARD M., *et al.*, 1972. *Licit and Illicit Drugs*. Boston: Little, Brown, 1972.

CALDERONE, MARY S., ed., 1958. *Abortion in the United States*. New York: Paul B. Hoeber, Inc.

CHAMBERS, MARIAN, 1973. "Ex-City Official Says He's Homosexual," *The New York Times,* October 3, 1973, pp. 1, 42.

Dealing With Drug Abuse: A Report to the Ford Foundation, 1972. New York: Praeger.

DELANEY, PAUL, 1973. "Legality Sought for the Numbers," *The New York Times,* September 7, 1973, p. 11.

DUSTER, TROY, 1970. *The Legislation of Morality*. New York: The Free Press.

ERIKSON, KAI T., 1962. "Notes on the Sociology of Deviance," *Social Problems,* 9 (Spring 1962), pp. 307–314.

FARBER, M. A., 1973. "Drug Traffic Thriving Despite New Stiff Law," *The New York Times,* October 8, 1973, p. 1.

FERRETTI, FRED, 1973. "Hard Drugs Face Hard New Law," *The New York Times,* August 26, 1973, p. E3.

GARFINKEL, HAROLD, 1956. "Conditions of Successful Degradation Ceremonies," *American Journal of Sociology,* 61 (March 1956), pp. 420–424.

GEIS, GILBERT, 1973. "Abortion and Prostitution: A Matter of Respectability," *The Nation,* September 3, 1973, pp. 179–180.

GEIS, GILBERT, 1972. *Not the Law's Business? An Examination of Homosexuality, Abortion, Prostitution, Narcotics, and Gambling in the United States,* National Institute of Mental Health, Crime and Delinquency Issues Monograph Series. Washington, D.C.: U.S. Government Printing Office.

GOFFMAN, ERVING, 1961. "The Moral Career of the Mental Patient," in Goffman, *Asylums.* Garden City, N.Y.: Doubleday Anchor Books.

GOLDBERG, PETER B., AND DELONG, JAMES V., 1972. "Federal Expenditures on Drug-Abuse Control," in *Dealing With Drug Abuse,* 1972, pp. 302–305.

HOLAHAN, JOHN F., 1972. "The Economics of Heroin," in *Dealing With Drug Abuse,* 1972, pp. 292–293.

HOROWITZ, IRVING LOUIS, AND LIEBOWITZ, MARTIN, 1968. "Social Deviance and Political Marginality: Toward a Redefinition of the Relation Between Sociology and Politics," *Social Problems,* 15 (Winter 1968), p. 282.

HUMPHREYS, LAUD, 1972. *Out of the Closets: The Sociology of Homosexual Liberation.* Englewood Cliffs, N.J.: Prentice-Hall, Inc.

KAPLAN, JOHN, 1971. *Marijuana—The New Prohibition*. New York: Pocket Books.

KITSUSE, JOHN I., 1962. "Societal Reactions to Deviant Behavior: Problems of Theory and Method," *Social Problems,* 9 (Winter 1962), pp. 247–256.

The Knapp Commission Report on Police Corruption, 1972. New York: George Braziller.

LADER, LAWRENCE, 1966. *Abortion.* Indianapolis: Bobbs-Merrill.

LADER, LAWRENCE, 1973. *Abortion II: Making the Revolution.* Boston: Beacon Press.

LEE, NANCY HOWELL, 1969. *The Search For an Abortionist.* Chicago: University of Chicago Press.

LINDESMITH, ALFRED R., 1967. *The Addict and the Law.* New York: Random House, Vintage Books.

LOFLAND, JOHN, 1969. *Deviance and Identity.* Englewood Cliffs, N.J.: Prentice-Hall, Inc.

MAY, EDGAR, 1972. "Narcotics Addiction and Control in Great Britain," in *Dealing With Drug Abuse,* 1972, pp. 345–394.

MILLETT, KATE, *et al.,* 1973. *The Prostitution Papers.* New York: Avon Books.

MORRIS, NORVAL, AND HAWKINS, GORDON, 1970. *The Honest Politician's Guide to Crime Control.* Chicago: University of Chicago Press.

NATIONAL COMMISSION ON MARIHUANA AND DRUG ABUSE, 1972. *Marihuana: A Signal of Misunderstanding.* The Official Report of the NCMDA. New York: Signet Books.

NATIONAL INSTITUTE OF MENTAL HEALTH (NIMH) TASK FORCE ON HOMOSEXUALITY, 1972. *Final Report and Background Papers.* Washington, D.C.: U.S. Government Printing Office.

PACKER, HERBERT L., 1968. *The Limits of the Criminal Sanction.* Stanford: Stanford University Press.

PRESIDENT'S COMMISSION ON LAW ENFORCEMENT AND ADMINIS- TRATION OF JUSTICE, 1967a. *Task Force Report: The Courts.* Washington, D.C.: U.S. Government Printing Office.

PRESIDENT'S COMMISSION ON LAW ENFORCEMENT AND ADMINIS- TRATION OF JUSTICE, 1967b. *Task Force Report: Narcotics and Drug Abuse.* Washington, D.C.: U.S. Government Print- ing Office.

PRESIDENT'S COMMISSION ON LAW ENFORCEMENT AND ADMINIS- TRATION OF JUSTICE, 1967c. *Task Force Report: Organized Crime.* Washington, D.C.: U.S. Government Printing Office.

QUINNEY, RICHARD, 1972. "Who is the Victim?" *Criminology,* 10 (Nov. 1972), p. 315.

REISS, ALBERT J. JR., 1971. *The Police and the Public.* New Haven: Yale University Press.

ROGERS, A. J., III, 1973. *The Economics of Crime.* Hinsdale, Ill.: The Dryden Press.

SCHELLING, THOMAS C., 1967. "Economic Analysis and Organ- ized Crime," in President's Commission, *Task Force Report: Organized Crime,* pp. 114–126.

SCHUR, EDWIN M., 1965. *Crimes Without Victims.* Englewood Cliffs, N.J.: Prentice-Hall, Inc.

SCHUR, EDWIN M., 1971. *Labeling Deviant Behavior.* New York: Harper and Row.

SCULL, ANDREW, 1972. "Social Control and the Amplification of Deviance," in Scott, Robert A., and Douglas, Jack D., eds., *Theoretical Perspectives on Deviance.* New York, Basic Books, pp. 282–314.

SKOLNICK, JEROME H., 1966. *Justice Without Trial.* New York: John Wiley and Sons.

SUTHERLAND, EDWIN, AND CRESSEY, DONALD R., 1960. *Principles of Criminology,* 6th ed. Philadelphia: Lippincott Co.

UCLA Law Review, 1966. "Adult Consensual Homosexual Behavior and the Law: An Empirical Study of Enforcement and Administration in Los Angeles County," *UCLA Law Review,* 13 (1966), exp. pp. 690–707.

WALD, PATRICIA M., AND HUTT, PETER BARTON, 1972. "The Drug Abuse Survey Project: Summary of Findings, Conclusions, and Recommendations," in *Dealing With Drug Abuse,* 1972, p. 28.

WICKER, TOM, 1973. "Gooks, Slopes, and Vermin," *The New York Times,* May 4, 1973, p. 37.

WILSON, JAMES Q., MOORE, MARK H., AND WHEAT, I. DAVID, JR., 1972. "The Problem of Heroin," *The Public Interest,* Fall 1972.

(WOLFENDEN) COMMITTEE ON HOMOSEXUAL OFFENCES AND PROSTITUTION, 1972. *Report,* Home Office, Cmnd. 247. London: Her Majesty's Stationery Office.

ZIMRING, FRANKLIN C., 1971. *Perspectives on Deterrence.* National Institute of Mental Health (NIMH), Center for Studies of Crime and Delinquency. Washington, D.C.: U.S. Government Printing Office.

A
PHILOSOPHER'S
VIEW

ARE THERE REALLY "CRIMES WITHOUT VICTIMS"?

by HUGO ADAM BEDAU

I
INTRODUCTION

Early in 1973, according to a report in *The New York Times,*

> The criminal justice section of the New York State Bar Association recommended . . . that all criminal sanctions be removed from a variety of "victimless" crimes, including possession or private use of small quantities of marijuana.
>
> The section . . . was nearly unanimous in its approval of resolutions on prostitution, public intoxication and marijuana use and possession . . .
>
> The section's resolution on marijuana said that the present penalties for possession threatened "the criminal prosecution of a significant portion of our population for engaging in a personal act which poses no demonstrable danger to the public."

The recommendation was for removal of all criminal penalties for "private use and possession of reasonable amounts of marijuana and treating the gift or profitless transfer of small quantities in a non-criminal manner."

Regarding prostitution, the section recommended repeal of the existing law and adoption of measures similar to the British Streetwalkers Act, which is directed principally against public solicitation. It also recommended nonpenal sanctions, such as counseling for first offenders convicted under the proposed law.

The section said criminal penalties for public drunkenness placed "an inappropriate burden on our overtaxed criminal justice system." It recommended "emergency treatment for intoxicated persons in public health facilities and the ending of the processing of these cases through the criminal courts and jails." (Montgomery, 1973)

At the present time, such recommendations as these by the New York State Bar Association are no longer novel. No doubt, if adopted into law, these reforms would bring much needed aid to our overextended and understaffed criminal justice agencies. By expanding the scope of personal freedom under law, these reforms would respect the rights of various minorities and, for that matter, of everyone to engage in deviant (atypical, abnormal) conduct. Indeed, "decriminalizing" (removing criminal penalties for) these activities seems long overdue if, as the *Times* report describes them, they are truly " 'victimless' crimes." However, this description, "victimless crimes," should give us pause. Is it really true that the use of marijuana, the condition of public intoxication, and the activity of prostitution involve no "victim," and for this reason it is absurd and wrong to make such things criminal violations which carry heavy penalties and lead to millions of arrests each year? Most generally, the issue is whether there really are crimes without victims. This question naturally leads to others. If there are crimes which are truly victimless, for what reasons did they come to be regarded as criminal in the first place? Does a crime become victimless only when no one at all is injured, or when no person other than the consenting participants are injured? Should crimes without victims be decriminalized altogether, or should the current severity of the punishments merely be reduced? On the other hand, if it is arguably false that these activities have no victims, how did the phrase, "victimless crimes," become so popular?

Some of these questions are more easily answered than others. The very concept of victimless crimes is of fairly recent origin. Not until the 1950s did one find leading American criminologists speaking of crimes such as gambling, prostitution, and drug abuse as offenses where "the 'victim' sides with the criminal in defiance of the law" (Sykes, 1956, p. 56), because in such offenses the "victim and criminal are linked in a symbiotic relationship" (p. 58). The idea that in these offenses *there is no victim at all* is already hinted at in those tell-tale quotation marks placed around the word "victim." Within the past decade, this notion has come out of the closet and the term "victimless crimes" is now in the lexicon of working criminologists, lawyers, civil libertarians, and journalists. The reasons are several and diverse. In recent years there has been much public agitation for law reform on abortion, homosexuality, and drug addiction, often led by those who identify themselves as participants in these activities. Concurrently, there has been a growing interest among criminologists to approach the study of all criminal offenses by examining the

victim-offender relationship, an approach which has spawned
the subdiscipline, victimology (Drapkin and Viano, 1974).
Thanks to the influential volume, *Crimes Without Victims*,
published in 1965 by my co-author in this volume, Edwin
Schur, the connection between law reform on abortion, homosexuality, and drug addiction, and the idea of victimless crime
was made explicit for professional audiences as well as the general public. In the last few years, a flood of essays and reports
has appeared on the themes of overcriminalization and decriminalization, the coercive enforcement of morals, paternalism,
and victimless crimes (for the most recent list of references,
see Geis, 1972, p. 255). Yet anyone who is willing to examine
closely these writings is entitled to come away somewhat dis-
satisfied. As I hope to show in the ensuing pages, the scholarly
authorities in criminology have been using a confused concept
of victimless crimes. Precisely, their definition seems to rely on
several distinct and non-coextensive criteria. As a consequence, it is very difficult to draw up a list in any definite or
uniform way of all and only those crimes which are victimless,
and to distinguish them from the crimes which do have victims.
Likewise, until the concept of victimless crimes is further
analysed, it is impossible to go through the penal code of any
jurisdiction and pick out all and only those criminal laws which
should be revised or repealed because they create victimless
crimes and authorize punishment for them. Yet, surely, these
were the false hopes implicitly created by the notion that we
can clarify and organize our thoughts, and penetrate the jungle
of the criminal law, by means of the notion of "victimless
crimes." Now, as I shall try to show, it is possible to construct
a more or less adequate definition of this idea and to make
some use of it in criminal law reform. However, to do this we
must rely on some theory or other of *basic human rights*. In

particular, we need to determine which rights-violations deserve absolute *prohibition* by the criminal law, which instead deserve only partial control through *regulation,* and which activities are not rights-violations at all, and therefore must be *tolerated* (see below, section VI). If I am correct, the search for answers to these questions will take us beyond sociology and criminology, and into moral philosophy. Only there can we find the necessary theory of human rights, which in turn sets the conditions for the calculation of the costs which society ought to pay in order to prohibit, regulate, or tolerate conduct of which most people disapprove.

II
VICTIMLESS CRIMES AND VICTIMIZATION

Let us begin by noticing the first warning sign of conceptual and theoretical trouble ahead: the authorities do not agree among themselves as to which crimes are victimless. Edwin Schur, as we noted earlier, initially singled out under this rubric only the crimes of abortion, homosexuality, and drug addiction (Schur, 1965, p. iii). The criminologist Jerome Skolnick mentioned private fighting and crimes of vice, such as gambling and smoking marijuana (Skolnick, 1968, p. 630), narcotics, abortion, homosexuality (p. 631), and prostitution (p. 632). The jurist Herbert Packer identified fornication, gambling, and narcotic offenses as victimless crimes (Packer, 1968, p. 151), but he also mentioned bribery and espionage in this category (p. 267). Norval Morris, criminologist and jurist, cited drunks, addicts, loiterers, vagrants, prostitutes and gamblers (Morris, 1973, p. 11) as persons who commit crimes without victims; he explicitly excluded abortion from his list (p. 62), although in his book with Gordon Hawkins, abortion was equally explicitly included among the crimes which "lack victims" (Morris and Hawkins, 1970, pp. 3, 6, 13–15).

For the sake of summary and easy comparison, Table I lists the range of criminal offenses which the authorities we have discussed have identified as victimless crimes. While this table omits the views of many others who have written on this subject with equal authority, it is representative and will suffice for our purposes. The reader must be careful not to infer from the absence of a checkmark that the authority listed would necessarily exclude the offense in question from the category of victimless crimes. This is particularly true in regard to the obviously related activities described here as "drug addiction," "marijuana use" and "narcotic use." All that may be inferred from such absence is that the offense was not explicitly discussed or described as a victimless crime in the source cited. Thus, much of the apparent disagreement in these lists is owing to nothing more than selective discussion and illustration. Finally, it is important to keep distinct the class of victimless crimes and the class of offenses thought to deserve decriminalization. True, the main interest of the concept of victimless crimes derives from its usefulness in decriminalization proposals. The two concepts, however, only intersect; neither coincides with nor includes the other. Packer's discussion of bribery and espionage shows that even if these two crimes are victimless in some sense or other, it would still be unreasonable to recommend that bribery and espionage cease to be punishable offenses.

TABLE 1. CRIMES WITHOUT VICTIMS

	Schur (1965)	Skolnick (1968)	Packer (1968)	Morris (1973)	New York State Bar Assn. Crim. J. Sec. (1973)
Abortion	X	X			
Bribery			X		
Drug Addiction	X			X	
Espionage			X		
Fornication			X		
Gambling		X	X	X	
Homosexuality	X	X			
Loitering				X	
Marijuana use		X			X
Narcotic use		X	X		
Private fighting		X			
Prostitution		X		X	X
Public drunkenness				X	X
Vagrancy				X	

One could multiply these lists indefinitely, but even this brief survey shows two things: (1) no two lists of crimes without victims are the same; and this suggests (apart from carelessness or deliberate selectivity by the authors quoted) that (2) the concept of victimless crime does not denote a stable class of offenses at all. One important reason for these two difficulties is that *victimization* is not a simple concept. It is quite possible for a person to fail to victimize someone in a violent or irreparable fashion, and yet to succeed in victimizing someone nonetheless. In order to appreciate the scope of the idea of victimization, it helps to have a brief catalogue of the ways in which one person can victimize another: (i) a person may lose life or limb through another's assault, (ii) a person may be physically harmed, but not irreversibly injured (maimed), by another, (iii) a person may cause another mental anguish, psychological trauma, by assault, threats, or taunts, with crippling or incapacitating results, (iv) a person may be exploited, degraded, manipulated, or debased by another, through isolated acts or established practices, (v) a person may have something imposed upon him, or taken from him, by another and without his own informed consent, (vi) a person may be deprived by another of something of value, e.g., position, status, reputation, influence, affection and esteem of others, (vii) a person's property or possessions may be lost or damaged through the malicious act of another.

What do all these kinds of victimization have in common? Nothing, at least, nothing physical, physiological, or psychological as the common and peculiar effect upon the victimized person. Trivially, we can say that all acts of victimization are acts in which one person does *violence* to another. But doing violence to a person is violating what? (See Shaffer, 1971.) If we are to make sense of victimization and the violence it involves as a common result of the above kinds of acts, we must say that in each sort of interaction listed above, a person normally (that is, a normal person with an understanding of his

own nature and environment) has an *interest* in *not* undergoing the experience, event, or interaction in question. In each
case, some *injury* (from the Latin for "injustice") would befall
him. Furthermore, we can say that society, through its govern-
ing agents and officers, has the duty to prevent the injury and
protect the interest. Such personal interests which warrant
societal protection are usually called *basic human* or *personal
rights* (see Melden, 1970, and Dorsen, 1971). The prevailing
political and legal theory on which our institutions are pro-
fessedly built is precisely the protection of such rights of persons. Indeed, from the theories of John Locke in the 17th
Century down to the latest pamphlets of the American Civil
Liberties Union, the whole rationale for government is unintel-
ligible apart from the belief that individual persons have rights,
and that impartial governmental powers are needed primarily
for the implementation and protection of these rights. More
needs to be said, of course, about the sources, nature, and possible conflicts of these rights. For the present, however, it suf-
fices to note that we cannot understand the diverse phenomena
which involve doing violence to another, victimization and injury, without ultimately appealing to an essentially moral doctrine of personal rights. Only in this way can we grasp the
common feature of the kinds of victimization there are.

To restate this in terms appropriate to our discussion, we
may say that a person has been *victimized* whenever any of his
or her *rights* have been *violated* by another; and that whenever
a person's rights have been violated through deliberate, malicious acts, he or she has been the *victim of a crime.* (No doubt,
a crucial factor in our assessment of such victimization will be
the degree to which the victim is judged to have brought the
injury on his own head, by provocation, solicitation, entice-

ment or avoidable acquiescence.) To believe, therefore, that one lives in a society where there are crimes without victims is to believe that there are offenses defined by law which involve no malicious or deliberate violation of anyone's rights by another. In order to determine whether this is true, it is necessary to have: (a) a theory (or at least a list) of the basic rights of persons, (b) a subset of these rights which it is appropriate to protect under the criminal law, viz., all those which when violated by deliberate and malicious acts of others cause personal injury, (c) a catalogue or check-list of the criminal offenses in the jurisdiction, and (d) a showing that some of the laws in (c) cannot be coordinated with any of the rights in (b). There, in a nutshell, is the task of criminal law reform organized around the idea of victimless crime, and presented in a way which gives due prominence to the role played by a theory of human or personal rights.

Now that we have a better grasp of the idea of victimization and injury, let us return to the prior point of considering the various proffered lists of crimes without victims, to see whether a person can be victimized by any of those activities. It may seem that I am about to belabor the obvious, but if the important first step is to see, as I believe it is, that criminologists do not agree in what they instance as a crime without a victim, then the important second step is to see that, once we understand the idea of victimization, many of these crimes in some instances (and some in most instances) involve a participant who is victimized by it. True, the harmfulness of some of these activities will depend on the age and health of the participant, e.g., fornication, smoking (marijuana or tobacco). In other cases, e.g., prostitution, the relevant question is whether the activity is degrading and whether it is injurious to engage in conduct which is degrading (see Women Endorsing Decriminalization, 1973). In a private fight, whether or not anyone is injured depends on what happens, nothing more and nothing less. In some cases, such as espionage, there may be no person injured, even though harm may be inflicted on a government and indirectly upon the society it serves. In the case of bribery, everything depends on what the bribed person has been bribed to do; he may harm others, but not invariably. In gambling, the harm to the gambler may be zero and in any case will vary depending upon his disposable income and other factors. As for drunkenness, public or private, there is little doubt that irreversible physical harm is brought upon the drunk by virtue of the alcohol he has consumed, irrespective of his consent or willingness to become and remain a drunk. The same is less true of drug abuse generally, and not all drug offenses involve narcotic or addictive drugs. The case of abortion is the most problematic, because whether or not anyone is harmed depends on whether the unborn fetus is to count as another person (or a living human being with rights) who is involved in the activity though incapable of consent. Loitering and vagrancy, however, seem to be wholly victimless offenses, even if they easily lead to offenses (trespassing, disturbing the peace) which are not.

This survey teaches us another lesson: nothing uniform about our lists of offenses is revealed when we examine them to see how the chief participant, the "victim," is situated or affected. The participant-as-victim is obviously involved in these activities in a wide variety of different ways. It would be most unfortunate if the new bit of jargon, "crimes without victims," were to cause us to be less sensitive to such facts, and to blur our perception of the ways in which persons can harm themselves and be harmed by others. There is some irony in this tendency, since criminologists have in recent years urged that it is important to know precisely who (if anyone) is victimized in any given criminal activity, and to what degree. The implication that there are a whole range of activities commonly made punishable as criminal offenses in which *no one is victimized* is, therefore, unfortunate.

III
THE PROBLEM OF DEFINITION

Let us turn now to attempts by criminologists to define the idea of victimless crimes. This requires us to examine the four major features in the offenses we have been discussing that have led criminologists and jurists to say these crimes involve no victims, or—as they sometimes say in qualification—no victims "in the usual sense of the word," or no "direct victims."

Edwin Schur remarks that the offenses he discusses (abortion, homosexuality, drug addiction) involve the *consent* of the parties involved to an exchange of prohibited goods or services, and that "the element of consent precludes the existence of a victim—in the usual sense of the word" (Schur, 1965, p. v). Let us call this the *consensual participation* feature of victimless crimes. Now it is true, as a general rule, that persons do not knowingly consent to engage in activities which do harm to themselves. But that is true only as a general rule. The problem, of course, is that not all harmful acts are like a gunshot or knife wound: some have a benign facade that conceals the eventual harmful effects on the participant. In the usual sense of the word, "victim," as defined by the typical current dictionary, a person is a victim *whenever* he is harmed or caused to suffer by any of the means discussed earlier (section II). The question of the cause or agency of harm is not at issue; nor are the questions of his consent and permission, his understanding and knowledge, nor the immediacy and proximity of the harm. Whether by virtue of his own act, that of another, or even of an impersonal agency (we do speak of victims of cancer), a person is to be judged a victim of *x* just in case *x* causes him to suffer, harms or injures him. The mere fact that a person consents to engage in a certain activity, without any further qualifications, does not entail that he is never harmed or caused to suffer by what he consents to—as the lives of thousands of alcoholics, addicts, gamblers and prostitutes testify.

The case of abortion presents obvious and special difficulties. If we are to think of abortion as a crime without a victim, and as an activity in which the participants give their knowing consent, then we must be thinking of the woman who is undergoing the abortion and the abortionist and their presumed relationship. But if abortion (at least at some stages in pregnancy, e.g., during the last trimester) involves killing an unborn, fetal *person,* it is obvious that the activity of abortion proceeds without the consent of one of the parties involved. It is also obvious that since in abortion (or, more strictly, aborticide), one party is killed, abortion always involves a victim, even though it involves no pain or suffering for that victim. If, therefore, abortion is going to be thought of as a victimless crime, then (to borrow from my analysis of the previous section) we must believe that *the fetus has no rights* which abortion violates. That may be so, but it has to be argued (see Feinberg, 1973c, and Hilgers and Horan, 1972). Abortion is a special case, however. The other examples suffice to show that, in general, it is not quite true that "the element of consent precludes the existence of a victim—in the usual sense of the word." To put it simply, *the class of activities to which all participants consent is not coextensive with the class of activities whose effects never harm or victimize the participants.* There is, however, another side to the story and it cannot be neglected. One would expect to encounter severe problems in preventing and deterring any class of acts where the participants in a position to withhold consent nevertheless do not do so. The presence of consent, therefore, bears less on the issue of victimization and more on the issue of enforceability. The legitimate public interest in the latter, however, should not blind us to the former.

This brings us to a second important feature often used to characterize this class of offenses. Jerome Skolnick has written that "by definition, crimes without victims are not reported . . ." (Skolnick, 1968, p. 631). Similarly, Morris and Hawkins comment that many "crimes lack victims, in the sense of complainants asking for protection of the criminal law" (Morris and Hawkins, 1970, p. 6). Let us call this feature of victimless crimes *the absence of complainant-participant*. The argument is, presumably, that since both parties are willing participants in the act, e.g., prostitution, the "victim" (the prostitute? her customer?) can be expected not to report the "crime" to the police. This failure to report offenses to the authorities, as many observers have pointed out, leads to various abuses and corruptions in the officials charged with criminal detection, arrest, prosecution, and conviction. Illegal searches and seizures, electronic surveillance, and entrapment, as well as police corruption and demoralization, and even police blackmail of the so-called "victim"—all these thrive on the seemingly futile attempts to enforce criminal penalties against deviance and vice. But we must be careful, and not try to prove too much. Not only so-called victimless crimes go unreported; many activities which indubitably inflict harm upon persons also go unreported by their victims. In the extreme case, it is obviously impossible for a victim of murder (or of any undiscovered crime) to report to the authorities that he or she has been harmed, but no one would argue that in such cases the murder is a crime without a victim. Gangland extortion, where a store owner may be threatened with severe property damage or personal harm if he reports the crime; embezzlement and employee pilfering, where the employer may find his insurance rates skyrocketing and his customer confidence seriously impaired; sexual assault and rape, where the woman victim is ashamed to submit herself to interrogation by cynical male police officers—these are merely the obvious examples which come to mind where, for quite different reasons, persons who know they have been harmed will not report their victimization to the police. In short, we cannot argue from the fact that an activity is not reported to the police to the conclusion that it involves no victim.

Another problem arises in the notion, expressed typically by Herbert Packer, that victimless crimes are those "offenses that do not result in anyone's *feeling* that he has been injured so as to impel him to bring the offense to the attention of the authorities" (Packer, 1968, p. 151, emphasis added). Let us call this the *self-judged harmlessness* of victimless crimes. Packer and others who believe that there is a category of crimes without victims also believe that we should allow the

question of whether someone has been victimized by engaging
in a certain activity to turn on how he or she "feels" about it
at the time. There are at least two obvious objections to such
a position. The first is that it tends to blur the general distinction between what a person *feels* (or, more accurately in these
cases, what a person believes to be true about himself) and
what *is true* about his state or condition. Those who agree with
Packer here verge on obliterating the distinction between
whether or not a person feels (or believes) that he has not
been harmed, and whether or not he has been harmed. We
may be inclined to think the generally valid distinction between what seems to be true and what is true has no application in such cases, because where the issue is whether a rational person—informed, conscious, mature—has been harmed
by some activity, he can safely be regarded as the final (or at
least as a competent) authority. Where a person himself is
judging his own condition or status (i.e., asks himself, "Does
doing x hurt me when I do it? Do I dislike doing x? Does
doing x leave me worse off than not doing x?"), we are inclined to adopt as a general policy that what a person feels
in regard to self-harm is a reliable index as to whether he has
been harmed. Yet it is not an infallible index, nor is it an
irrebuttable presumption of fact. It is not even reliable except
on the assumptions already indicated, viz., that the person
has an informed, mature grasp of exactly what he is doing,
and of what its effects will be upon his life opportunities and
capacities, so that it can be said of him that he is not acting
in ignorance or otherwise foolishly, carelessly, injuring himself
contrary to his opinion at the time.

The second important objection to blurring the general distinction—merely because we have the agent judging his own

activities—between feeling unharmed and being unharmed, is that social policy has traditionally reflected our belief that in certain classes of cases society needs to be protected from people who willingly take risks for themselves and others. Laws designed to provide such protection are often confused with "paternalistic legislation," and accordingly are condemned, but this is a mistake (Dworkin, 1971). The point can be seen in certain kinds of risk-taking where normal, healthy adults are involved, e.g., operating dangerous machinery. In such cases, we require that the persons engaged in these activities use safety equipment, take rest periods, have regular physical check-ups, etc. We can understand these requirements as paternalistic, but there is a better alternative. They can be understood as attempts to reduce the likelihood of self-injury which are imposed on an unwilling society by persons who are unmindful of the personal risks and social costs involved in serious accidents. In a significant variety of other cases, involving infants, juveniles, the mentally ill or deficient, we readily adopt and defend paternalistic policies because we do not want the law to use as its criterion of criminal harm the self-judgment of the persons involved that they do not "feel" they take unreasonable risks or believe that they have been injured by the activity. But even if we are inclined to let the law use this criterion for the conduct of consenting adults, it may well be in spite of and not because of a belief that the person involved cannot be harmed when he or she feels unharmed. Why we should adopt such legal policies for the conduct of adults remains to be seen. As I shall try to show below (section IV), the search for this reason takes us into further consideration of the theory of personal rights alluded to earlier (section II).

The fourth and final feature of victimless crimes can be called their *transactional* or *exchange* nature. As Schur puts it, abortion and the other victimless crimes involve "the willing exchange of socially disapproved but widely demanded goods or services" (Schur, 1965, p. 8), "the willing exchange, among adults, of strongly demanded but legally proscribed goods or services" (p. 169). There can be no doubt that this aspect is one which is highly relevant to law enforcement and law reform because of the way gambling, prostitution, and drug addiction become sources of vast illicit (and untaxed!) revenues. Their illegality has little effect in reducing the large clientele for these "goods or services." Even so, despite the merits of bringing to bear an unsentimental economic viewpoint on the kinds of offenses under review, much is left out or distorted in this perspective. Prostitution and gambling may well deserve the kind of emphasis this approach yields, but most of the other victimless crimes exhibit a transactional or economic exchange structure, only incidentally, if at all. Homosexuality, for example, essentially involves two or more persons; but unlike prostitution it need have no economic overtones. Narcotic abuse and drug addiction only incidentally involve more than one person; theoretically, a person can manufacture and use illegal and harmful drugs in complete solitude. Abortion does or does not essentially involve an interpersonal relationship, depending on whether one thinks of this act with reference to the unborn fetal person or only with reference to the abortionist and his client-patient. Vagrancy and loitering have no exchange or transactional character at all, and public drunkenness has one only incidentally.

We have been examining four different criteria in terms of which criminologists and others have tried to characterize a class of crimes they call "victimless." In order of discussion, the criteria have been: consensual participation, absence of a complainant-participant, self-judged harmlessness, and transaction or exchange. Precisely how criminologists view these four criteria is somewhat unclear. Obviously, the four criteria are not coextensive; therefore none can be treated as a sufficient condition of victimless crimes, unless the others are to be eliminated. The natural step is to treat these criteria so that each is regarded as a necessary condition, and then to combine them as the sufficient condition for the class of victimless crimes. Doing that results in the following definition:

> An activity is a victimless crime if and only if it is prohibited by the criminal code and made subject to penalty or punishment, and involves the exchange or transaction of goods and services among consenting adults who regard themselves as unharmed by the activity and, accordingly, do not willingly inform the authorities of their participation in it.

It is tempting to comment on the interrelation of the four criteria used in this definition. Absence of a complainant-participant appears to be an empirical consequence of consensual participation and self-judged harmlessness. Consensual participation and self-judged harmlessness, however, seem to explain each other, depending on the context. Proper as such abstract conceptual questions are to any rigorous critique of a definition, let us put aside any further discussion of them here. Instead, let us notice two major difficulties which emerge from this discussion for the theory of victimless crimes.

The first problem is that this definition is quite incapable of subsuming the dozen or so offenses we have seen are to be found on lists of victimless crimes. The definition is too nar-

row, in that it excludes abortion and vagrancy, public drunkenness and crimes such as bribery and espionage; the lists of
victimless crimes with which we began are simply too inclu-
sive. There is no convenient remedy for this. The only alternative is to reject one or more of the four essential characteristics of the concept of victimless crime; such a redefinition of
the concept would render it ill-fitted to the actual discussions
and issues out of which it originated. It is better to conclude
simply that perhaps some activities currently against the law
are similar to, but not exactly like, some other activities which
truly are victimless crimes.

The second and more interesting consequence is that the
idea of harmlessness or victimlessness has a very tenuous relation to the crimes covered by this definition. The presence
of the four defining attributes of victimless crimes simply cannot guarantee, either conceptually or empirically, that every
such crime is harmless to the participants. We have seen earlier
(section II) that there is at best only a loose empirical connection between consensual participation and self-judged harmlessness, on the one hand, and actual harmlessness and non-
victimization on the other. It is, therefore, misleading for
criminologists and law reformers to argue on behalf of reducing or eliminating the criminal penalties for abortion, prostitution, etc., by implying that these activities are harmless and
victimless. About all they can legitimately argue, given the
definition of victimless crimes—a definition which does not
explicitly or implicitly contain the idea that these activities are
always harmless!—is that if any participant is harmed or injured by abortion, prostitution, etc., then he or she has *no
ground for criminal complaint* against the other participants.
The reason is that more or less informed consent by all parties

was a condition of engaging in the activity in the first place, and such consent always bars any subsequent complaint. (This is the idea behind the ancient legal maxim *volenti non fit injuria,* that harms which befall a person as a result of acts to which he consented are not injuries or violations of his rights.) Not only that. There is the further tacit assumption that if the participants in the activity consent to it and judge themselves unharmed by engaging in it, nobody else can be injured by it, either; and if that is so, society has no right to interfere by prohibiting the activity and subjecting it to penal sanctions.

We have here in these new considerations what in fact is the main thing, from a moral point of view, to be said on behalf of law reform in the area of so-called victimless crimes. We have seen how there is no guarantee that can be given on behalf of the harmlessness of an activity to the participants simply by conceding that the activity is consensual and is judged by the participants to be harmless at the time. Now, we have uncovered a deeper point, one which can perhaps be best expressed by the following argument:

1. Society and government should allow persons to engage in whatever conduct they want to, no matter how deviant or abnormal it may be, so long as (a) they know what they are doing, (b) they consent to it, and (c) no one— at least no one other than the participants—is harmed by it.

2. In activities such as abortion, gambling, public drunkenness, etc. (a) and (b) and (c) are all true.

3. Therefore, abortion, gambling, public drunkenness, etc. are victimless activities and the laws which make them criminal should be repealed.

As we have seen, the sole proof for premise 2 is provided by the judgment of those who engage in the conduct at the time of their involvement. The judgment of disinterested spectators or rueful self-judgment at a later date is presumed to be irrelevant, or at least not decisive. We can see this most clearly if we amplify the point in terms of the notion of rights-violation used in section II to define the notion of victimization. It can be argued that in so-called victimless crimes, even if harm does accrue to one of the participants, he is not really a victim of a crime, because by freely consenting to engage in the illegal activity in the first place, the participant waives any further moral right to declare that his rights have been violated by the harm (it turns out) he has suffered. It is time now to consider what can be said for relying on a principle such as the one embodied in premise 1, since its consequences for our topic turn out to be so significant and far-reaching.

IV
LIBERALISM AND DECRIMINALIZATION

The philosophical source of this important principle is to be found in the famous essay, *On Liberty,* written by John Stuart Mill over a century ago. The essence of Mill's position is expressed in these two passages:

> [T]he sole end for which mankind are warranted, individually or collectively, in interfering with the liberty of action of any of their number, is self-protection. That the only pur-

pose for which power can be rightfully exercised over any member of a civilised community, against his will, is to prevent harm to others . . . The only part of the conduct of any one, for which he is amenable to society, is that which concerns others. In the part which merely concerns himself, his independence is, of right, absolute. Over himself, over his own body and mind, the individual is sovereign . . . As soon as any part of a person's conduct affects prejudicially the interests of others, society has jurisdiction over it, and the question whether the general welfare will or will not be promoted by interfering with it, becomes open to discussion. But there is no room for entertaining any such question when a person's conduct affects the interests of no persons besides himself, or needs not affect them unless they like . . . In all such cases, there should be perfect freedom, legal and social, to do the action and stand the consequences. (Mill, 1859, pp. 135, 205–206)

In these words, Mill has asserted, as he said, a "principle . . . to govern absolutely the dealings of society with the individual in the way of compulsion and control." Others have called it, somewhat pretentiously, Mill's Principle of Legitimate State Interference. For brevity and ease of reference, we can call it *liberalism.*

Mill thought his liberalism to be "a very simple principle," but in this (if the subsequent debate over the past century proves anything) he was wrong (see Stephen, 1874; Hart, 1963; Devlin, 1965; Wasserstrom, 1971). There are a host of threshold uncertainties in his doctrine. Who is to count as a "member" of society? Who are the "others" whose "interests" always deserve to be taken into account? How do we tell what is in a person's "interests" and what "harms" them? How are we to identify that "part" of a person's "conduct" which

"merely concerns himself?" There are classic questions and
they have been much discussed (Pennock & Chapman, 1962;
Radcliff, 1966). A person's "interests" are mainly whatever
does interest him, but at times they will include also whatever
ought to interest him (whether or not it does so), given the
conditions of his self-development and happiness. By "harm,"
Mill does not mean only (though, of course, he means mainly)
bodily harm. But the merely offensive or annoying is not in
itself harmful. By "the others" in question, Mill means primarily identifiable, assignable individuals who can come forward and point to themselves as persons whose interests have
been adversely affected or violated by someone's conduct; the
claims of unborn future generations play no role in Mill's
thinking (even if they can without much distortion be covered by his principles). By "members of society," Mill means
(as he rather quaintly puts it) "human beings in the maturity
of their faculties." Children and those who are properly the
wards of others are explicitly excluded from the reach of his
liberal principles. Finally, it is important in evaluating Mill's
doctrine to distinguish actual harms from the possibility or
the threat of harm, and to translate all threats of harm against
society and its values into threats against identifiable individuals and their interests.

    With these preliminary clarifications behind us, we can turn
to the burden of Mill's liberalism. It is clear from his argument's context that he believes there is a strong presumption
in favor of the finality of any adult person's judgment about
what he does and does not like, want, or find harmful. As
Mill says, "with respect to his own feelings and circumstances,
the most ordinary man or woman has means of knowledge
immeasurably surpassing those that can be possessed by any-

one else" (Mill, 1859, pp. 206–207). Like most other liberals, Mill believes that if you are a normal, adult person,
then you are a competent judge of your own desires and of
their consequences for you. Similarly, he believes that others
are in the best position to inform you when your desires and
their consequences affect them adversely. Mill is famous for
his individualistic and egalitarian undergirding of the Principle of Utility; as he puts it, "everybody to count for one,
nobody for more than one." He should be equally famous for
the individualism and egalitarianism of his belief that each
person is the best judge of what he really wants, desires, likes
—and in that sense, of his own interests. On the plausible assumption that no one wants or likes to harm himself, and that
each person believes he knows when he is harming himself,
it follows (and Mill accepts the implication) that what a person voluntarily chooses to do does not harm him. In extreme
cases there will be exceptions, of course, but this is the general
rule. Even if harm does accrue to the individual, when no
one else is harmed society has no right to interfere. Thus, the
moral principle used in the first premise of the argument
at the conclusion of the previous section is entailed by the liberal Principle of Legitimate State Interference which Mill
formulated and his heirs defend.

What, if anything, keeps liberalism from being an arbitrary
moral norm? On what ground can such a moral principle as
Mill's be justified? Without a lengthy philosophical excursus,
it is not possible to answer this question in any convincing
fashion. We should note that, for his own part, Mill seemed to
rest his case not only on the Principle of Utility, but also on
the values, as he put it, of "the free development of individual-
ity" and of "individual spontaneity"; he believed all thoughtful

persons would agree that these characteristics of human life had "intrinsic worth" (Mill, 1859, p. 185). The fact that the "intrinsic worth" of "individual spontaneity" is not obviously compatible with his utilitarianism need not trouble us. Other philosophers, especially those more at home in the tradition of Rousseau and Kant, might put Mill's conviction in another way. They would insist that his idea of the intrinsic worth of human freedom is correct, but that it is better expressed as the doctrine of equal human dignity, and that this is an ideal value which is shared both by the moral principles which create our ordinary duties and by those moral principles which guide our highest moral aspirations (cf. "the morality of duty" and "the morality of aspiration," Fuller, 1964, pp. 5–9). Through reflection and personal experience we come to appreciate the desirability of maximizing our own personal freedom insofar as that is compatible with non-interference in the freedom of others. The most elaborate and impressive recent attempt to justify such a principle is to be found in the influential philosophical treatise, *A Theory of Justice,* by John Rawls. He has defended as the first and fundamental principle of justice that "each person is to have an equal right to the most extensive basic liberty compatible with a similar liberty for others" (Rawls, 1971, p. 60). As he shows, underlying such a principle is a vision of the basic equal dignity of all persons, a moral vision which has infused Western religion and philosophy down through the centuries. Given Rawls's quite general formulation of the first principle of justice, Mill's liberalism emerges as a corollary. Mill, I think, would have understood and accepted this. In any case, we can see in this brief sketch how an attempt to justify a liberal Principle of Legitimate State Interference would force us on to considerably more philosophical reflection than is contained in Mill's own somewhat perfunctory allusions to the "intrinsic worth" of "individual spontaneity."

Once it is granted that a course of activity does not harm the participants, as evidenced by their own willingness to engage in it, and if it cannot be shown to be harmful to others, the proponent of liberalism is committed to the conclusion that the conduct in question must not be prohibited under law. Mill knew that in his own day such a doctrine was well in advance of public sentiment and in sharp contrast to the prevailing criminal codes then in force in most civilized countries. To illustrate the practical consequences of his position, he showed how his reasoning would require the repeal of all laws to enforce Sunday closing and all laws to punish fornication, gambling, public drunkenness, and even polygamy. In such cases, Mill argued, the sole ground of legitimate prevention— the evidence of harm to others—was absent. Thus, the prohibition by law of the conduct was morally indefensible. As Mill also recognized, his position could be formulated in terms of a notion of inviolable personal rights. Each person has an "absolute right" to engage in any conduct he or she pleases, so long as it does not violate the equally absolute right of others to be free of harmful invasions of their privacy. The only apparent exception to this which Mill discussed was the freedom to contract into slavery. He argued, in a way reminiscent of Kant, that it is illogical and self-contradictory to invoke a principle of inviolable personal rights against the interference of others in order to defend conduct which yields, as Mill knew chattel slavery does, the total loss of all personal rights. As he succinctly put it, "The principle of freedom cannot require that [a person] . . . should be free not to be free"

(Mill, 1859, p. 236). In thinking that only free contracts into slavery violate his liberalism, Mill may underrate (as we shall see in the next section) the idea that other kinds of activity may, more subtly, have much the same effect in the long run. Mill is simply not troubled by the possibility that the conduct in which a consenting adult engages today may turn out to have irreversibly damaging consequences for him tomorrow. He thus comes close to embracing the doctrine that "man has an inalienable right to go to hell in his own fashion" (Morris & Hawkins, 1970, p. 2).

Mill's liberalism gives us a moral basis as valid in our day as it was in his for reforming the criminal code. In its results, it would be more or less equivalent with the reforms recommended by lawyers, criminologists and others who today rely directly on the notion of victimless crime. From a moral point of view, however, there is a profound difference. When Morris and Hawkins, for example, argue on behalf of decriminalizing victimless crimes, the nature of their argument is essentially that the social costs of continuing to treat these activities as illegal far exceeds the social benefits, and that although decriminalization is not without its costs, too, the overall balance much favors that alternative. Although they do not use the jargon of cost/benefit analysis, with its morally neutral coloration and its atmosphere of scientific rigor, this is what their emphasis on the social cost of overcriminalization amounts to. Consider, in this light, the six objections they marshal against victimless crimes: (i) "the criminal law operates as a 'crime tariff' which makes the supply of such goods and services profitable for the criminal"; (ii) this in turn helps to create and finance "large-scale criminal groups," a vast underworld of commercialized crime; (iii) the crime tariff also has a "secondary criminogenic effect," since it is only by such violent and victimizing offenses as robbery, theft, burglary, and arson that poorer people can raise the money they need to pay for these illicit goods and services; (iv) a whole "criminal sub-culture" is fostered by causing addicts, gamblers, prostitutes, etc., to associate with each other; (v) an enormous "diversion and overextension" of relatively scarce police resources results from the attempt to repress such criminal activity; (vi) because the participants are willingly engaged in their illegal activity, the police must resort to bribery and other forms of corruption to secure arrests and indictments (Morris & Hawkins, 1970, pp. 5–6).

Throughout this catalogue of social ills spawned by victimless crimes, there is no explicit reference made to any moral principles of justice, rights, or freedom. This is not necessarily owing to any oversight, much less to cynical disbelief in such principles. It more likely stems from the calculated belief that no uniform policy recommendations can be reached where moral convictions are allowed any prominence in the argument. Perhaps it arises from a search for morally neutral factual generalizations around which persons of divergent moral convictions can agree. Whatever the explanation, the perspective is at odds with the one provided us by Mill. Not that philosophers and social scientists contradict each other here; it is quite possible to argue from liberalism or from a cost/benefit analysis of overcriminalization and come up with the same law reform proposals. Rather, it is that philosophers and social scientists tend to reason from very different considerations. To philosophers, it is likely to appear that the social scientists mistakenly think either that a cost/benefit analysis has no tacit moral assumptions at all, or (equally

mistakenly) that its tacit moral assumptions—invariably some
form of utilitarianism—are somehow superior to those which
involve basic personal rights. (For an excellent discussion of
this conflict by a social scientist, though not on the issue of
decriminalization, see Titmus, 1971, pp. 195–246; for a useful
philosophical debate, see Smart and Williams, 1973.) A philosopher is thus likely to argue that the rational basis for
decriminalization of gambling, prostitution, and other such
activities lies ultimately in such moral principles as those of
Mill (or Rawls); second, that this moral judgment is reinforced by the social cost analysis provided by social scientists
such as Morris and Hawkins; and, finally, that the willingness
of social scientists to rest their law reform proposals on a
cost/benefit analysis is either irrational or else tacitly relies
in the end on the validity of moral principles substantially
equivalent to liberalism.

V
PATERNALISM AND MORALISM

Arrayed against a policy of decriminalization of victimless
crimes based on the moral principles of liberalism are three
types of objection. The first concedes the relevance of Mill's
liberal principles but contends that prostitution, gambling and
the rest in fact cause harm to others which is ignored or under-
rated by law reformers, and therefore even on their own assumptions they should support rather than oppose the con-

tinued application of the criminal law to these activities. Although this position is respectable and is not obviously false, it has little or no support from the social scientists who have studied victimless crimes in the United States in recent years. Homosexuality, abortion, prostitution, narcotic drug abuse, and gambling are the prime examples of victimless crimes, and to those who have most carefully studied the facts from all sources, subjecting these activities to criminal punishments as is done at present can only cause society more harm and misery than would be caused by decriminalization (for the most recent and complete survey, see Geis, 1972). This first objection to decriminalization, therefore, is not very persuasive given the available evidence. Rather more interesting, because they apparently reject the moral principles of liberalism, are the other two objections, *paternalism* and *moralism*.

By *paternalism* is meant here the imposition through the criminal law of constraints and incentives in order to protect a person from himself, and thus to use as the justification for curbing a person's freedom of conduct the argument that (a) it is for his own good in the long run that he refrain from engaging in activities which have harmful consequences for him, and that (b) his ready consent to engage in these activities despite such consequences is based on inadequate information, irrational assessment of that information, or weakness of willpower and self-restraint. Mill, in the context of his initial formulation of liberalism, explicitly singled out paternalism for criticism. After his remark that "the only purpose for which power can be rightfully exercised over any member of a civilized community, against his will, is to prevent harm to others," he immediately added, "His own good, either physical or moral, is not a sufficient warrant" (Mill, 1859, p. 135).

Paternalism is not necessarily frowned upon in all circumstances, however. It is deemed by Mill and most liberals since his time to be a perfectly appropriate basis for parental policies toward the conduct of their young children, and by the community generally toward the conduct of anyone who is by nature abnormally impulsive, ignorant, dull, or infirm. No sensible defender of decriminalizing victimless crimes would advocate abandoning the traditional protections which the criminal law has provided for children and juveniles against exploitation, manipulation, and injury at the hands of adults. The classic instance of this is the crime of statutory rape. Society has long decreed that a young woman's consent to sexual intercourse shall not be a bar to prosecution of the male as though he had taken her by force and without her consent, provided she is below the statutory age limit, e.g., 16 years old. What is in dispute, therefore, is paternalistic legislation as it affects the conduct of normal, consenting, and moderately well-informed adults.

The chief argument against decriminalizing victimless crimes from this perspective goes like this: (a) Contrary to liberalism, a person's own good, either physical or moral, is "a sufficient warrant" for state interference with his or her conduct; status as an adult and the act of voluntary consent do not make this principle inapplicable; (b) many victimless crimes, as we have already seen (section I), in fact often cause subtle and deferred harms to one or more of the participants, even when it is conceded that their crimes may be substantially harmless to the rest of the community; therefore (c) decriminalization for such offenses is contrary to sound public policy and moral principle.

Critics of the above argument must be careful not to try to prove too much. It is difficult to deny that there is much paternalistic legislation in our society, that it restricts the conduct of consenting adults, and that not all of this legislation should be repealed. For example, consider the laws which require motorcyclists to use safety helmets, automobiles to have seat belts, persons with religious scruples (e.g., Christian Scientists) to accept life-saving blood transfusions, and laws which forbid duelling, swimming at public beaches when no lifeguard is on duty, usurious and unregulated interest rates on loans (Dworkin, 1971, pp. 108–111). All these are instances of well-founded paternalistic legislation. An attack on the paternalistic critique of decriminalizing drug abuse, gambling, and homosexuality is in some danger of discrediting the paternalism which seems legitimate enough in these other areas. What liberal reformers need, from a moral point of view, is some basis for paternalism which does not require an acceptance of paternalism across the board.

Whatever may be true historically, it is certainly possible to rest a defense of paternalism on the claim that it is a principle in the service of, and not contrary to, the spirit of liberalism. This is what the philosopher Gerald Dworkin does when he argues that "Paternalism is justified only to preserve a wider range of freedom for the individual in question" (Dworkin, 1971, p. 118). This, after all, was the basis of Mill's own argument against honoring the decision of an adult to contract into slavery. It is also the basis for the legitimacy of paternalistic policies toward children, the mentally ill, the senile, etc. If, therefore, an adult consents to some activity and society proposes to interfere with his or her freedom to

act in this way, the burden is on those who favor the restrictive, paternalistic legislation to show that the activity in question really is harmful and dangerous to the participants and
that if the would-be participant were fully informed about the
consequences of participation and took a reasonably prudent,
self-interested view toward his or her own life, then the person
would accept the legislation as a reasonable restraint on conduct. That is a rather complex and demanding criterion, but it
is easily applicable to the laws, for example, which require
motorcyclists to wear safety helmets (and it could be a basis
for similar legislation to require drivers of automobiles to use
safety belts). It does not take any imagination or scientific investigation to establish that fatal results are likely to result
from almost any motorcycle accident if the rider has no adequate helmet. In such cases, we can defend the imposition of
paternalistic interferences as a kind of "insurance policy"
which society takes out to deter anyone from making decisions
which are "far-reaching, potentially dangerous and irreversible" (*Op. cit.*, pp. 122–123). With the exception of abortion
—always a special case in our discussion because of the de-
fenseless fetus involved—the argument for decrimalization of
some victimless crimes (especially gambling, homosexuality,
and prostitution) is not impeded by these concessions to paternalism. Everything, however, does depend on the facts, the
true effects on the biology, physiology, and psychology of
individual adults who engage in these activities. Much of the
dispute over reforming the narcotic and drug abuse laws turns
on what, precisely, the effects of long-term usage are. Even
the most ardent paternalist is likely to doubt the wisdom of
keeping the manufacture and sale of heroin—to cite only the
most extreme case—an unlawful activity (indeed, one punish-

able in some jurisdictions by death), if he believes, after careful study of all the data, that the "steady use of opiates over a long period of time likely would not produce untoward physical sequelae" in the user (Geis, 1972, p. 131).

But paternalism is not the only ground on which decriminalization of victimless crimes is resisted. We can see this plainly enough in the historic example of the national experiment with the prohibition on the manufacture and sale of intoxicating liquors from 1920 to 1933. No doubt it is true, as a fact of medical science, that the continued use of large amounts of alcoholic beverage is harmful because it results in irreversible physiological damage. Enthusiasts for Prohibition half a century ago could, therefore, bring forward this paternalistic ground for the legislation they favored. But it was fulmination from the pulpits of America, preaching the sinfulness and not just the harmfulness of Demon Rum, that helped to bring about Prohibition. Likewise, the recent laws which restrict the advertising (though not the manufacture or sale) of cigarettes have a similar paternalistic basis in medical fact, even though an earlier generation was warned to stay away from tobacco not primarily on these grounds. It is hardly surprising, therefore, that masses of statistical data assembled by teams of qualified social scientists today do not wholly suffice to persuade the public to decriminalize victimless crimes. The regulation under law of liquor and tobacco, and the traditional total prohibitions on homosexuality, prostitution, and gambling are in large part rooted in something other than the principle of paternalism. That further principle is *moralism,* the third of the basic objections to the liberal argument for decriminalization.

By *moralism* is meant here the policy of using the criminal

law to curb a person's freedom of action not on the ground
that it is unfairly harmful to others (for this is already prohibited by liberalism), nor on the ground that it is an irrational
harm to the participant (this is already prohibited by paternalism), but solely on the ground that it is offensive, degrading,
vicious, sinful, corrupt, or otherwise immoral. Moralism easily
degenerates into the arbitrary imposition of a majority's professed principles of conduct upon the deviant conduct of minorities. Even at its best, moralism necessarily involves extensive invasions of privacy. At its worst, it smacks of blue-
nosed intolerance and aggressive Puritanism of the sort made
notorious during the past century by Anthony Comstock in
New York and by the Watch and Ward Society in Boston
(thanks to the latter, the verdict, "Banned in Boston," was
once the guarantee of large audiences for a spicy play and of
big sales for a racy book). The keystone of the moralist's
argument against decriminalizing victimless crimes is that
these activities are morally wrong. Lord Patrick Devlin, perhaps the most influential and candid recent spokesman for
moralism and author of the much discussed book, *The Enforcement of Morals,* has phrased it this way: "society has a
prima facie right to legislate against immorality as such"
(Devlin, 1965, p. 11). The moralist typically believes that
"it is not possible to set theoretical limits to the power of the
State to legislate against immorality . . . The suppression of
vice is as much the law's business as the suppression of sub-
versive activities . . ." (*Op. cit.,* pp. 12, 13–14). As for the
scope and definition of immorality, "for the purpose of the
law, it is what every right-minded person is presumed to consider to be immoral . . . If the reasonable man believes that

a practice is immoral and believes also . . . that no right-minded member of his society could think otherwise, then for the purpose of the law it is immoral" (*Op. cit.*, pp. 15, 22–23). Every society largely consists of "a community of shared ideas on politics, morals, and ethics" (*Op. cit.*, p. 10), and it cannot exist for long without preservation of its "public morality" through the agencies of the criminal law.

Anyone imbued with liberalism will simply note its incompatibility with moralism, and proceed to reject the latter and move on to other questions. Social scientists who believe that a cost/benefit analysis of social policy either has no moral foundations or has foundations superior to moralism, will do the same. Most of the criticism fired at moralism has come from these directions (Hart, 1963; Wooton, 1963; Wasserstrom, 1971). Once again, however, we must note the danger of trying to prove too much in attacking moralism. As Louis B. Schwartz, co-author of the Model Penal Code of the American Law Institute, has rightly noted, "Virtually the entire penal code expresses the community's ideas of morality, or at least of the most egregious immoralities" (Schwartz, 1962, p. 86). There is no reason to balk at this; there is also no reason to think it is an argument for moralism. Murder, assault, rape and other such crimes of personal violence are morally outrageous. No one has the right to do such things to others, and such immoralities as these unquestionably deserve denunciation, prohibition and punishment through the agencies of the criminal law. No opponent of moralism could reasonably disagree with this. But murder and the rest are obviously the kind of *harmful* immoralities which Mill's liberalism was designed to prohibit; therefore there is no need whatever to turn to the vague and extravagant claims of moralism in order to base the penal code on "the community's ideas of egregious immorality." What is in dispute is whether *harmless* immoralities—conduct deemed corrupt or immoral, but not harmful to anyone not engaged in it and harmful to the participants in so doubtful and obscure a fashion that they readily give their consent to take the risks—are to be prohibited by the criminal law. That is the sole issue presented by the claims of moralism.

Among various objections to the moralist's position, two deserve mention here. First, the moralist is simply in error if he thinks that abortion, gambling, homosexuality, prostitution and narcotic offenses are rare and infrequent deviations in a society whose manifest and prevailing "public morality" effectively condemns such activity. Whatever may have been true in the past, nothing so simple is true today, at least in the United States. At the very least, the plain evidence of the growth in known abortions, for example, once "abortion on demand" became legalized in New York, along with the support this change in the law received from many religious and other ethically responsible groups, shows that abortion is no longer morally unacceptable to large numbers, even a majority, of adult Americans today (Geis, 1972, pp. 97–99). Essentially the same is true of the change in attitudes toward marijuana. The moralist's objection, therefore, is particularly vulnerable because it tends to proceed on the false assumptions that the moral attitudes toward abortion and the rest are fixed and unchanging and that the conventionally proclaimed attitudes really govern private conduct. Even if they did, the moralist's views are subject to a second objection. What, after all, is the source of legitimacy and authority for the moral

principles which repudiate conduct harmless to non-partici-
pants and which require that such conduct nevertheless be prohibited by the criminal law? If the practice of abortion and the
rest do in fact cause harm to society, then liberal (or liberal
plus paternalistic) principles suffice to condemn the practice
and no sane reformer would seek to change the law. If, however, the only harm decriminalization of these activities would
cause are changes in individual conduct and in the prevailing
attitudes toward that conduct, then this is not truly a harm at
all; it is merely the effect of repudiating old values and the
evolution of new social practices. To make such harmless
conduct unlawful is to give to traditional beliefs a protection
and an advantage in influencing conduct they do not deserve.

Finally, we should note that both paternalists and moralists,
in their dissatisfaction with liberal principles, share a common
belief that the criminal law is not only a useful but a legitimate
and necessary instrument of moral education, because it provides a unique incentive to prudent and elevated conduct. But
is this really true? It does not take an anarchist, who would
repudiate all coercive legal institutions, to see that some matters are best left to the extra-legal institutions in society. The
criminal justice institutions are not the only facilities and
powers which a society has at its disposal to influence and
alter individual conduct which would otherwise fall short of
some appropriate moral standard. Surely, the best argument
for invoking the criminal law against a given pattern of conduct is that, otherwise, innocent and non-consenting persons
will be injured and harmed by the deliberate and callous dis-
regard of their interests by others. Likewise, the worst argument for bringing the criminal law to bear on a person's conduct is that, otherwise, the persons in question will lack the

negative incentives of the criminal sanction to be as good, healthy, and rational as they ought to be.

VI
THE REGULATORY APPROACH

Let us return now for a closer look at the recommendations of the New York State Bar Association regarding marijuana, prostitution and public drunkenness (recall section I). We see that while they are prepared to recommend abandonment of the traditionally *prohibitive* posture of the criminal law for various offenses, they are by no means ready to adopt a thoroughly *permissive* posture. To put this in terms of the previous discussion (sections IV–V), they are ready to repudiate moralism—but not ready to embrace liberalism. Large bulk sales of marijuana would presumably still be in violation of some criminal statute or other; at least, no reform of the penal law is proposed affecting the profitable transfer of quantities of marijuana. Similarly, public solicitation by prostitutes and pimps would remain a criminal offense. Only in the case of public drunkenness is a wholly non-punitive, therapeutic approach adopted. Yet even here, the proposed curative regimen is not simply available but mandatory. With regard to all three crimes, therefore, the Bar Association recommendations opt for a policy neither of prohibition nor of permission, but of *regulation*. This is extremely important to notice, since it is the posture overwhelmingly preferred today by almost all public spokesmen on the issue of decriminalizing victimless crimes.

Although it is true, as Norval Morris has reminded us, "It is impossible to regulate behavior that you prohibit" (Morris, 1973, p. 11), one might still wonder why—apart from the need to placate entrenched moralists—the behavior in question must be regulated at all.

The reasons for regulation in the area of victimless crimes is well illustrated in two important but quite different examples. One is in the policy underlying the American Law Institute's Model Penal Code. As explained by Schwartz, the regulatory approach of the Code may be seen in its punitive provisions on prostitution. Schwartz concedes that, so far as he can see, "the patron's guilt is equal to that of the prostitute, but it is the seller rather than the sinful customer who is labelled a criminal" (Schwartz, 1962, p. 102). Under the Code, the patron can at most be convicted of a non-criminal "violation." The prostitute, however, can be convicted of a "petty misdemeanor" and sentenced up to thirty days in jail. Only the procurer can be convicted of a "third degree felony" and receive up to five years in prison. The approach of the Model Penal Code is clear; as Schwartz puts it, "the higher the rank in the selling organization, the graver the penalty" (*loc. cit.*). The same regulatory approach to many other victimless crimes can also be found regarding, e.g., the use, possession, and sale of marijuana (Geis, 1972, pp. 170–171).

As a second illustration of the regulatory approach, consider the Supreme Court decision in the important abortion case of *Roe v. Wade*. Mr. Justice Blackmun, writing for the Court, declared that so far as the Constitution is concerned, the states may pass legislation "regulating" abortion. Although a woman's decision to abort a pregnancy may not be absolutely prohibited, it is permissible for the states to impose regulations by statute insofar as the regulation "reasonably relates to the preservation and protection of maternal health" (*Roe v. Wade*, 1973, p. 732). For example, the abortion may be required to be performed by a doctor duly authorized to practice, as determined by the normal licensing procedures of the state, and the abortion may also be required to be performed in medical facilities (though not necessarily a hospital) also licensed and regulated by the state.

The theories underlying these two examples of regulation are quite different. In the case of abortion, the regulatory approach is imposed by the Court because, simple though abortion may be in the early stages of pregnancy, it can easily become a dangerous and complex medical undertaking, which requires all the skill of a competent obstetrical surgeon and the supporting facilities of a fully equipped clinic or hospital, if the pregnant woman's health is not to be risked or impaired. Here, it is the *dangerousness* of the activity which invites regulation of its exercise, even though presumably the abortion in question is not decreed by the state but desired by the woman. In the case of prostitution, however, it is the *offensiveness* of the conduct, and especially of procuring—the commercialization of vice—which prompts the increasing scale of punitiveness recommended by the Model Penal Code. It seems clear that the draughtsmen of the Code would stamp out prostitution if they could; nothing of a similar sort is implied by the Court's decision on abortion. (Opponents of abortion no doubt regard it as offensive. But this is unimportant and derivative. What counts, in their view, is that abortion involves the "murder" of an "innocent" human being.) Yet what is true of the recommended law on prostitution is typical of the way many so-called victimless crimes are viewed by current law reformers. Why is this so? Is it because, although no one is harmed by these activities, public prudishness cannot be prudently ignored? Or is it that although persons are harmed by these activities, they are not harmed very much? Or is it that although the participants are harmed rather severely in some cases, they consent to it anyway, so that it is really futile to try to prevent them from engaging in such practices and one must be content to penalize solicitation, with its often flagrant presentation of the alluring aspects of the conduct? (Thus, when the Supreme Court upheld the prison sentence for publisher Ralph Ginzburg, it was not because the pictures and essays in his magazine, *Eros,* were particularly offensive. What the Court found to be in violation of the federal obscenity statute was the "pandering" and "commercial exploitation" of sex which the defendant used in order to stimulate the market for his magazine; see *U. S. v. Ginzburg,* 1966.) Whatever the explanation, there lies at the root of the proposal to regulate such conduct the belief that someone, the reformers, their clientele, the typical state legislature, does not approve of the conduct in question, and that this disapprobation has a sound basis in principle.

But what is that principle? It may be nothing more novel than the paternalism or moralism we have already discussed. It also could be some form of the idea that various verbal and non-verbal activities can cause *offense* to persons (as obscene telephone calls and exhibitionism offend some women) by virtue of flouting deeply held convictions, and that in being offensive these activities are *harmful* or something sufficiently akin to harmfulness as to be virtually indistinguishable from it (Feinberg, 1973a). The exact formulation of such a principle, however, has so far proved to be extremely difficult, even for philosophers (Bayles, 1973, and Feinberg, 1973b). As things currently stand, there is small likelihood of such a principle being generally understood and serviceable as a basis of law reform for those who wield political power in state and federal legislatures. Those who favor the regulatory approach, therefore, are left in the uncomfortable position of relying on a principle to justify interfering with privacy and liberty of conduct which either has not yet been satisfactorily articulated by anyone, or else is a disguised version (whether out of conviction or out of a spirit of political compromise) of paternalism or moralism.

That is not all. In the case of the regulatory approach typified by the Model Penal Code's position on prostitution (though apparently absent from the Court's position on abortion), we encounter a further difficulty. It is not one to be much stressed by philosophers, perhaps, but it should give pause to those who pride themselves on their political realism. The Model Penal Code, we are told, reflects the desires of many of us not to attempt to "regulate private sexual behavior"; but the Code is "not . . . so hesitant in prohibiting the commercialization of vice" (Schwartz, 1973, p. 91).

> This is a lesser intrusion on freedom of choice in personal relations. It presents a more realistic target for police activity. And conceptually such regulation presents itself as a ban on a form of economic activity rather than a regulation of morals (*loc. cit.*).

But in proposing to penalize brothel keepers with up to five years imprisonment, this approach surely has at least two unwelcome features. One was well expressed by Mill, when he said that "the fact of following anything as an occupation, and

living or profiting by the practice of it, cannot make that criminal which would otherwise be admissible" (Mill, 1859, p.
232). The other difficulty is that the regulatory approach almost entirely fails to deal with the problem of the crime tariff,
since it supplies a powerful motive to those with the greatest
economic incentive in prostitution to use their economic power
to stay in business and out of prison. There may be little to be
said in favor of throwing prostitutes and their patrons into jail;
but it is hard to see how anyone concerned with the political
realities will be able to believe that the regulatory approach
will appreciably reduce the spread or the scale of "commercialized vice," or that it will do anything more than tempt and
corrupt the police and the courts.

In sum, the regulatory approach may be less disastrous morally and sociologically than the prohibitory approach, but it
has its own dangers. The dubious morality of paternalism and
moralism can be avoided only by relying on a principle of interference concerning the harmfulness of offensiveness that no
one has adequately formulated. It invites an aggravation of the
problem of official corruption by adopting a frankly economic
or tax-like approach to its scale of sanctions. For these reasons,
I am rather more inclined to agree with the advice of the sociologist Gilbert Geis, who concludes his recent study, *Not the
Law's Business?*, with the counsel that "the most efficacious
method of dealing with deviancy is to ignore, to the furthest
point of our tolerance, those items which we find offensive"
(Geis, 1972, p. 261). Public drunkenness, prostitution, narcotics offenses, abortion, as well as pornography and obscenity
(two offenses almost entirely ignored in this essay)—these and
many other activities may be a stench in the nostrils of the
Almighty and an offense to those whose moral principles forbid

such conduct. But so long as they harm only those adults who knowingly and willingly choose to engage in such practices and are harmless to others, it is hard to see why the criminal justice system should be used to try to prevent and to punish those who want to do them. Let the hospitals take care of the sick, whether drunks or addicts or victims of automobile accidents or cancer. Let the police concentrate on protecting us from the injuries and violence which would be inflicted on us by a small minority. As for the rest, let us leave it to the control and guidance of education and persuasion, free of coercive criminal sanctions altogether.

VII
CONCLUSION

One final lesson to be learned from the study of victimless crime is the disturbing inconsistency with which our society proceeds in this area. Why, for example, do we allow persons to gamble with their money, so long as they spend it on some risky ventures (the stock market), but prohibit them if they wish to spend it on others (offtrack betting, the numbers pool)? Why do we license the sale of some personal services (escort services, massage parlors) and not others ("massage parlors," prostitution)? Why do we allow some demonstrably harmful substances to be sold without prescription and merely tax them (tobacco, alcohol) whereas some others (marijuana, cocaine) are unavailable over the counter at all? Why do we rush to pass paternalistic legislation in some areas (the statutory requirements of motorcyclists to wear safety helmets) and ignore it in others (the actual use of automobile safety belts required by law to be installed in new cars)? The list of such paradoxes is endless. The explanation in every case is ideological or historical, not logical or moral. What these paradoxes show is that our society allows victimization through the silence of the law, and that it is extremely difficult and perhaps impossible to find a sound principle or principles which will show that the current pattern of the law is a rational one.

My purpose in this essay has been only partly to attack over-criminalization and the legislation of morality. Rather, it has been to show that the concept of victimless crimes has theoretically unsatisfactory features which make it a less than perfect analytical category in terms of which to assess a variety of political, scientific, and moral questions related to the issue of decriminalization. People are, after all, often harmed in such crimes. Persons often give uninformed consent to their own participation in activities, ignorant of the consequences harmful to themselves which in due course will appear. The interest of individuals, in short, both of the participants and of others, may well be violated by many so-called victimless crimes. We can no more conclude from these facts that such conduct must be prohibited by vigorous enforcement of criminal sanctions against perpetrators, regardless of the cost, than we can accept the opposite conclusion, that society must bear these harms and violations of rights in silence. In a more constructive vein, I have tried to show that familiar principles of liberal social philosophy, stemming from Mill, give us a much sounder basis for understanding what is wrong with trying to enforce morality through the criminal law. We can avoid moralism altogether and paternalism where it is inappropriate by relying on a conception of human beings which accords to each of us an inviolable privacy, a freedom from legitimate state interference. And we can leave to sober public discussion and private reflection the difficult question what is to be done with and for those who have engaged in immoral conduct that harms themselves after all.

REFERENCES

BAYLES, MICHAEL D., 1973. "Comments: Offensive Conduct and the Law," in Care and Trelogan, 1973, pp. 111–126.

CARE, NORMAN S. AND THOMAS K. TRELOGAN, eds., 1973. *Issues in Law and Morality*. Cleveland: The Press of Case Western Reserve University.

DEVLIN, PATRICK, 1965. *The Enforcement of Morals*. London: Oxford University Press.

DORSEN, NORMAN, ed., 1971. *The Rights of Americans: What They Are—What They Should Be*. New York: Pantheon Books.

DRAPKIN, ISRAEL AND EMILIO VIANO, eds., 1974. *Victimology*. Lexington, Mass.: D. C. Heath and Company.

DWORKIN, GERALD, 1971. "Paternalism," in Wasserstrom, 1971, pp. 107–126.

FEINBERG, JOEL, 1973a. " 'Harmless Immoralities' and Offensive Nuisances," in Care and Trelogan, 1973, pp. 83–110.

FEINBERG, JOEL, 1973b. "Reply," in Care and Trelogan, 1973, pp. 127–140.

FEINBERG, JOEL, ed., 1973c. *The Problem of Abortion.* Belmont, Calif.: Wadsworth Publishing Company.

FULLER, LON L., 1964. *The Morality of Law.* New Haven, Conn.: Yale University Press.

GEIS, GILBERT, 1972. *Not the Law's Business? An Examination of Homosexuality, Abortion, Prostitution, Narcotics, and Gambling in the United States,* National Institute of Mental Health, Crime and Delinquency Monograph Series. Washington, D.C.: U.S. Government Printing Office.

HART, H. L. A., 1963. *Law, Liberty and Morality.* Stanford, Calif.: Stanford University Press.

HILGERS, THOMAS W. AND DENNIS J. HORAN, eds., 1972. *Abortion and Social Justice.* New York: Sheed & Ward.

MELDEN, A. I., ed., 1970. *Human Rights.* Belmont, Calif.: Wadsworth Publishing Company.

MILL, JOHN STUART, 1859. *On Liberty.* Reprinted in Mary Warnock, 1962, pp. 126–250.

MONTGOMERY, PAUL, 1973. "No Penalty Urged in Victimless Crimes." *New York Times,* January 28, 1973, p. 34.

MORRIS, NORVAL, 1973. "Crimes Without Victims: The Law Is a Busybody," *New York Times Magazine,* April 1, 1973, pp. 10–11, 58–62.

MORRIS, NORVAL AND GORDON HAWKINS, 1970. *The Honest Politician's Guide to Crime Control.* Chicago: University of Chicago Press.

PACKER, HERBERT L., 1968. *The Limits of the Criminal Sanction.* Stanford, Calif.: Stanford University Press.

PENNOCK, J. ROLAND AND JOHN W. CHAPMAN, eds., 1962. *Liberty: Nomos IV.* New York: Atherton Press.

RADCLIFF, PETER, ed., 1966. *Limits of Liberty: Studies of Mill's On Liberty.* Belmont, Calif.: Wadsworth Publishing Company.

RAWLS, JOHN, 1971. *A Theory of Justice.* Cambridge, Mass.: Harvard University Press.

Roe v. Wade, 1973. *Supreme Court Reporter,* 93 (Feb. 15, 1973), pp. 705–763.

SHAFFER, JEROME A., ed., 1971. *Violence.* New York: David McKay Company.

SCHUR, EDWIN M., 1965. *Crimes Without Victims: Deviant Behavior and Public Policy.* Englewood Cliffs, N.J.: Prentice-Hall, Inc.

SCHWARTZ, LOUIS B., 1962. "Morals Offenses and the Model Penal Code," *Columbia University Law Review,* 63 (1962), pp. 669–686, reprinted in Wasserstrom, 1971, pp. 86–106.

SKOLNICK, JEROME H., 1968. "Coercion to Virtue: The Enforcement of Morals," *Southern California Law Review,* 41 (1968), pp. 588–641.

SMART, J. J. C. AND BERNARD WILLIAMS, 1973. *Utilitarianism For and Against.* Cambridge, England: Cambridge University Press.

STEPHEN, JAMES FITZJAMES, 1874. *Liberty, Equality, Fraternity.* Edited by R. J. White and reprinted by Cambridge University Press, 1967.

SYKES, GRESHAM M., 1956. *Crime and Society.* New York: Random House.

TITMUS, RICHARD M., 1971. *The Gift Relationship: From Human Blood to Social Policy.* New York: Pantheon Books.

U. S. v. Ginzburg, 1966. *United States Reports,* 383 (1966), pp. 463–501.

WARNOCK, MARY, ed., 1962. *John Stuart Mill: Utilitarianism, On Liberty, Essay on Bentham.* Cleveland: The World Publishing Company.

WASSERSTROM, RICHARD A., ed., 1971. *Morality and the Law.* Belmont, Calif.: Wadsworth Publishing Company.

WOMEN ENDORSING DECRIMINALIZATION, "Prostitution: A Non-Victim Crime?" *Issues in Criminology,* 8 (Fall 1973), pp. 137–162.

WOOTON, BARBARA, 1963. *Crime and the Criminal Law.* London: Stevens and Sons.

THE
SOCIOLOGIST
COMMENTS

by EDWIN M. SCHUR

It should be clear from the preceding essays that there are at least several fairly distinct perspectives one might adopt in assessing the appropriateness of various provisions of the substantive criminal law. To some extent this is a matter of disciplinary preference. Sociologists always focus on those aspects of a problem that they consider most relevant sociologically, as philosophers emphasize those aspects most germane to philosophical concerns. But, here at least, the presence of multiple perspectives also reflects the very real complexity of the issues posed by what some term victimless crime. Not only do the behaviors involved give rise to intriguing legal, philosophical, and sociological questions, but frequently one or another of these "problems" is said to pose significant dilemmas for religion, medicine, or psychiatry as well. With such diverse orientations on hand, it is hardly surprising that the question of victimless crime continuously evokes debate and yet staunchly resists neat resolution.

Another, somewhat paradoxical, indicator of the topic's complexity is the fact that one's perspective for analyzing these matters need not fully determine one's policy recommendations. Indeed it must be apparent that while Professor Bedau and I approach the general question of victimless crime from strikingly different vantage points, we may nonetheless arrive at similar conclusions with respect to a number of specific legal provisions. What we disagree considerably about, however, is the mode of reasoning by which such conclusions are to be reached. Incorporated in this disagreement seem to be divergent understandings of the basis of the argument favoring decriminalization, the kinds of evidence relevant in assessing the appropriateness of specific uses of the criminal law, and the possibilities and mechanisms for determining "morality" and "truth."

To comment first on a relatively minor point, Bedau argues at some length that various analysts have used the term "victimless crime" in different ways (i.e., to cover different "offenses"), and that this is some indication the concept is faulty. Even if this variation were not (as he himself admits is the case) largely due to "selective discussion and illustration," it is difficult to see how the mere existence of such variation (in different treatments) could have much bearing on our evaluation of any one clearly stated use of the concept. (Virtually all concepts, after all, are susceptible of different interpretations and applications. To consider this a fatal flaw would in effect rule out the very process of conceptualization.) I believe that in fact there is a good deal more common ground among the users of the term than Bedau suggests. But at any rate, the meaning adopted here (the one that seems to be absolutely central) has been quite explicitly stated: victimless crimes arise when the attempt is made to ban by criminal law "the exchange between willing partners of strongly desired goods or services." It is this consensual exchange feature that lies at the heart of the argument for decriminalization, and often critics fail to appreciate fully its significance.

As we have already seen, the (unintended) empirical consequences of attempting to ban such exchanges are in large measure predictable. Furthermore, such consequences can be expected to follow *regardless* of any judgment we might choose to make as to whether individuals engaged in the transactions (or others) are "harmed" or "victimized." A focus on this element of wished-for transaction is the common thread running through the several varying analyses of victimless crime. There is no gainsaying that the word "victimless" has diverse connotations, and that in some ways an alternative concept (such as "complainantless crime") might more sharply and unequivocally highlight the key point. But referring to victimless crime does have the merit of drawing our attention to the participants' desire for the goods or services in question and the low probability, therefore, that they will complain about getting them. To that extent, what Bedau terms "self-judged harmlessness" is indeed a significant operative element in these situations.

Now it may be a legitimate question for empirical research whether, or in what degrees and ways, participants in such transactions really consider the behaviors harmless and themselves unvictimized. But the evidence is overwhelming that they rarely consider themselves sufficiently victimized *through the transaction* to wish it undone or the other participants punished. That certain outside observers may consider these attitudes undesirable or unwise surely in no way alters the empirically determinable consequences or concomitants of legal proscription. It is hard to see (as I shall stress further below) how one can make a moral or policy assessment of these situations without taking into account the social reality that constitutes them.

Another reason why the notion of victimlessness proves troublesome has to do with understanding the precise part it plays in the argument favoring decriminalization. Much of Professor Bedau's discussion appears to presuppose that proponents of decriminalization treat victimlessness itself as a direct criterion for moral choice or policy decision. I believe this represents a serious misreading of their position (or at least of my own). Proponents of decriminalization are not in fact primarily arguing that these "crimes" should be abolished because they are victimless. Rather, they are saying that the laws in question produce more social harm than good, and that a major reason for this is the victimless nature of the alleged "offenses." In other words, they are treating victimlessness (and its consequences) as an empirical *datum* (to be taken into account in evaluating the laws), *not* as a moral criterion. To argue, then, that victimlessness is not a good criterion for assessing laws is somewhat beside the point. The criterion being employed is not victimlessness as such, but extent of social harm. Therefore, unless the concept of social harm itself is to be challenged, the legitimate dispute seems really to center on the means of determining such harm—and in particular the relevance to such determinations of the kinds of empirical data alluded to above.

Obviously this problem (which in some respects is similar to or a version of that of determining "justice," or "the good society") has much occupied analysts of diverse persuasions and given rise to numerous schools of thought. For our purposes, it would seem best to concentrate on the specific issue of how to determine which behaviors ought to be proscribed by criminal law. Yet the disagreement between Professor Bedau and myself even on this matter appears to involve more general methodological differences. In considering how to reach these determinations, we tend to support our reasoning by recourse to different kinds of evidence, and we also appear to make different kinds of claims regarding the standing of our conclusions.

To say (as Bedau does at one point) that advocates of decriminalization may be searching for "morally neutral factual generalizations" seems to me rather misleading. A more accurate picture of their goal, I believe, would be conveyed by the phrase "morally relevant factual generalizations," for the claim underlying their approach is precisely that the moral judgments called for in these situations cannot be made without reference to the relevant facts. For his part, Professor Bedau appears here to be treating moral questions and factual questions as somehow residing in two quite distinct and mutually exclusive domains, a separation I consider to be unwarranted. His analysis seems indeed to require some system of "factually neutral moral generalizations," the search for which certainly seems laudable but the nature and validity of which remain to be established.

In determining what kinds of evidence are relevant to the making of specific moral judgments, we would do well always to have clearly in mind just what it is that we are judging. As I understand it, the debate about victimless crimes and decriminalization primarily concerns the morality of particular laws, rather than the morality of the proscribed behaviors.

Thus, for example, it is "the morality of making abortion a criminal offense," and not "the morality of abortion" that is most crucially at issue in this controversy. While it may be difficult to adequately address either of these questions without at least considering the other, it must be emphasized that proponents of decriminalization are in fact not asserting (to use the same example) that "abortion is moral," but rather they are in effect saying that "laws against abortion are immoral" (because, on the basis of available empirical evidence, such laws appear to be associated with greater social harm than would exist in their absence).

This is not to claim that the morality of abortion laws, or of any other laws, can be scientifically determined. It is simply to insist that the morality of specific laws must be assessed by weighing the claims of (inevitably) competing values, and that in this process one must take into account available evidence concerning the laws' actual operation. Just as there is little basis for believing in a completely "value free" social science, so too would the assertion of a "fact free" moral science be untenable. Perhaps it is revealing that when Professor Bedau gets around to evaluating specific legal policies (as in his discussion of the "regulatory" approach), he finds himself compelled to attend to the apparent behavioral consequences of such policies. Yet in other parts of his analysis he often seems to treat such considerations as being quite irrelevant to the "moral" issues.

The attempt to develop a scheme of abstract moral principles to guide legal policy decisions invariably runs the risk that its specific applications will involve the imposition of absolutist (some would say arbitrary) moral norms. Although Bedau at some point refers to "the dubious morality of paternalism or moralism," much of his argument seems to veer in the direction at least of the former if not also the latter. Surely his extensive effort to derogate the notion of "self-judged harmlessness" only makes sense if in fact he believes that it may be legitimate to curb individual freedom in order to protect people from themselves. Nor is his suggestion that there is a domain of legitimate paternalism persuasive.

The analogy to regulatory "protective" legislation in industry and elsewhere (e.g., motorcycle helmet laws) is a poor one. Such analogy would be more clearly to the point if in fact the decriminalization argument rested merely on the issue of harm to self or others. But as we have seen, the case for abolishing vice laws rests on a large body of evidence that the laws themselves produce substantial social harm. To the extent safety regulations are deemed acceptable, it is because they are seen as producing (overall) more good than harm.

At the same time, it is indicative of the slipperiness of paternalistic rationales that protective legislation earlier believed to be "in the best interests of women," is now being condemned as an infringement of their basic rights. Similarly, many analysts now are questioning the paternalistic assumptions underlying the once readily accepted "individualized" treatment of juvenile delinquents. In the context of the present discussion, Bedau's reference to the prohibition experiment (as somehow illustrating the legitimacy of paternalism) can only be described as ludicrous. Indeed, prohibition was (and continues to be cited as) the classic case of creating, and being unable to enforce, a victimless crime law. Presumably Bedau intends here to indicate that at times people do feel a need to pass paternalistic legislation. But that is beside the point. There is a rationale behind the creation of any law (almost always including "laudable" motives on someone's part), yet our concern here must be not simply with such motivations but also (and more crucially) with the consequences of criminalization. High principles are deceiving; needless to say, much evil has been done in their name.

According to my co-author, it is only in moral philosophy that we can hope to find a theory of human rights or interests that will permit us to determine when we should enact criminal laws and when we should not. While the search for such a theory can only be viewed as commendable, it is far from clear that (even if we could agree on the theory) it could be expected to resolve, for once and for all, the issues surrounding decriminalization. Again, it is in its application to specific instances that a general scheme of this sort is inclined to bog down. Without doubt, good people everywhere favor the fullest implementation and protection of basic human rights. The problem is that often they will disagree as to what such rights are, and how to protect and implement them. Expanding one person's rights often involves limiting another's; one person's liberty will be construed by others as license. In highly complex situations—the abortion debate springs to mind—there may well be disagreement even as to *whose* rights are at stake.

I find nothing in Professor Bedau's discussion that persuades me "moral philosophy" uniquely enables us to surmount such difficulties. It is true that abstract reasoning can help us to appreciate the complexity involved in decision-making, and can (if we choose to follow its dictates) promote consistency of rules and uniformity of application. But it can neither tell us what our goals (short-term or long-term) should be, nor establish the weights to be attached to the diverse elements that must be assessed in reaching specific decisions. No matter how convinced we may be that the judgment we make in a particular instance is called for by our overarching scheme of general principles, there is no getting around the fact that it is a *judgment,* and indeed that it is a judgment based on *our* scheme of principles.

As this comment may suggest, Professor Bedau and I differ greatly in the claims we would make for our respective orientations. Not only does his analysis at times depict "morality" in a highly abstract (and therefore, to me, rather empty) way, but furthermore he seems convinced that moral judgments (perhaps even his own moral judgments?) can be "true," and that there are not insurmountable obstacles to determining when this is so. These points are interrelated, for it must be his confidence in arriving at the truth (through abstract reasoning) that permits him at times to argue as though empirical data (enforceability of these laws, and the like) somehow reside "outside" the domain in which moral decisions are reached. That Bedau and I hold to very different conceptions of the nature of truth will be evident if one reconsiders his critical discussion of self-judged harmlessness.

Arguing that pro-decriminalization spokesmen erroneously accept the participants' own views as to whether they have been victimized, Bedau refers to a tendency "to blur the general distinction between what a person *feels* (or, more accurately in these cases, what a person believes to be true about himself) and what *is true* about his state or condition." Unfortunately he tells us nothing about how we would ascertain this "truth" or, if we could do so, just what it would represent. For most social scientists at least, statements such as "X is victimized" simply can never be demonstrated to be "true" or "false." To term someone "victimized" is to engage in quite a different sort of operation than to say he "has a broken arm" or that he "has red hair," or "is six feet tall." In the latter instances, one can apply widely accepted criteria to establish whether what the person believes to be true about himself and what "is true" (at least according to generally accepted standards) coincide or are discrepant. No such criteria or standards exist regarding "victimization." On the contrary, to "find" victimization is really to judge, to impute, to evaluate, to make a moral assessment. In the absence of universal moral consensus, there can be no adequate way of describing such judgments as being "true" or "false."

Unless one subscribes to some thoroughgoing conception of natural law, it would seem that the realities of life in a culturally (and morally) pluralistic world should cause one to be extremely cautious about implying a basis for moral certitude. Professor Bedau's apparent resistance to adopting a starkly relativistic conception of morals (a conception that admittedly has its own serious pitfalls) seems to push him toward a position in which he must make excessive claims for "moral philosophy." In saying this, I certainly do not mean to suggest that social science can provide the "solution" to these problems. Rather, that while philosophers, sociologists, and others can contribute to our understanding of them, ultimately value choices must be made (and will be made) and such choices cannot be "proven." Arguments can be presented, premises indicated, and evidence marshalled; but the most we can reasonably hope for out of this is that we might ourselves become increasingly convinced of the rightness of our conclusions, and that we might persuade others to accept them. At times Professor Bedau appears to want not only (at least for philosophers) a say in criminal law decision-making, but he also would like to invest such decisions with "truth." Naturally, all of us who express judgments on these matters would be pleased to view our judgments as "true"; but unfortunately, wishing won't make it so.

Where does this leave us with respect to the question of victimless crime? It should be reiterated that the case for decriminalization rests on the conclusion of many informed observers that the laws in question produce, on balance, more harm than good. At least in part because they attempt to control consensual transactions, such laws do little to deter proscribed behavior, they criminalize many otherwise law-abiding individuals, they encourage secondary crime and invite corruption, and they tend to undermine the general integrity of the legal system. One aspect of this that we would hardly sense from Bedau's discussion is that victimless crime laws create much human misery. Indeed Bedau's analysis scarcely mentions people, only principles. Yet the very point of such principles, after all, is that they should provide people with some guidance in their dealings with other people.

The only normative guideline that I would state regarding recourse to the criminal law is geared to keeping its uses to a minimum. Following the Wolfenden Committee and the working group of the American Friends Service Committee, I would insist that the law should be employed only when there is evidence that its use is likely to produce more good than harm, and I would place the burden of showing this on those who would advocate its employment. In making these assessments, neither abstract moral principle nor social science data-collection alone can provide a definitive basis for decision. With respect to the former, it is worth keeping in mind that the challenge to victimless crime laws has most directly arisen out of real-world situations that many people have found seriously disturbing, and not simply out of a belief that the laws violate some general principle of morality. This should suggest to us that the actual workings of such laws must be taken into account in assessing their merit. At the same time, no amount of empirical evidence can uncontrovertibly "establish" what decisions ought to be reached in these situations. Anyone choosing to (or called upon) to express a judgment on criminalizing or decriminalizing a particular kind of behavior should indeed weigh all the available evidence. But there remains no way of avoiding the personal value leap between the totality of that evidence and the making of a specific policy recommendation.

The position expressed here admittedly embodies a rather "political" conception of the nature of law. Just as people rarely appear in Bedau's analysis, neither does political action receive much attention there. Yet, as I noted earlier, large numbers of people who have been directly oppressed by victimless crime laws are taking broadly political action to overturn such laws and to redefine the social meaning of the currently proscribed behaviors. I would argue that this is not an unusual occurrence, but rather a particular kind of reflection of the fact that all laws emerge out of contests between competing definitions of reality (or, more legalistically, definitions of "rights" and "interests"). In a society displaying great sociocultural diversity, value competition or conflict is likely to be high. And under conditions of rapid social change, such as we have recently been experiencing, this conflict (always latent) increasingly may come to the fore.

We would of course like to believe that our legal system incorporates rules and mechanisms for transcending or at least dealing with such conflicts effectively in the interest of the common good. Yet we are all sufficiently aware of major gaps between professed legal ideals and the real workings of the law that few sensitive observers today would be inclined to consider any substantive legal provisions sacrosanct. For a variety of reasons which have now been presented in some detail, victimless crime laws produce a distortion of the functions of the legal system, placing it in the role of victimizer rather than protector or facilitator. No analysis, however principled, that fails to consider the social context within which these laws operate, can hope to do "justice" to the diverse facets of the victimless crime controversy.

THE
PHILOSOPHER
REPLIES

by HUGO ADAM BEDAU

Before turning to the major points of disagreement between Professor Schur and me, it is worth noticing that, in addition to our predictable divergence in emphasis and approach, which no doubt derives from our professional background and preferred modes of inquiry, we also seem to differ in something less tangible but no less important: roughly, how we view the entire issue under discussion. Schur seems to me to view the problem presented by victimless crimes as one which is ultimately rather simple, whereas I view it as one which is inescapably quite complex. Many of the substantive issues which obviously trouble me—of definition, personal rights, overriding normative commitments—cause him little or no worry at all. What seems to me necessary caution and thoroughness in analyzing these elements of our common subject seem to him to be needless embroidery. Whereas I see the route we must take to reach a sound policy on decriminalization of abortion, prostitution, and the rest, as a difficult and

somewhat uncertain one, fraught with a wide variety of un-
answered questions, he seems to see it as a straight one fully
illuminated all the way.

Some may attribute this global difference between us to our
temperament or idiosyncrasy, and dismiss it as irrelevant. I
think it is a revealing symptom of our quite different and pos-
sibly incompatible ways of reasoning about the entire subject.
To some extent, no doubt, this difference may be understood
as the result of an approach which relies mainly on empirical
generalizations and sociological data, in contrast to one in
which abstract analysis and philosophical criticism is upper-
most. Be that as it may, it is not obvious what, if any, resolution or synthesis can be hoped for. So we might as well plunge
into exploring some of the major differences between us in
detail.

Let us begin with the vexatious matter of definition. I realize
that philosophers since Socrates have shown what others regard
as a fetish for definition and a misplaced belief in the clarity
and rigor it is supposed to bring to any discussion. It is not
surprising, therefore, that Professor Schur is not concerned
either to comment on my efforts in defining victimization and
victimless crimes, or to provide a definition of his own which
measures up to the usual standards. It is interesting that in his
opening remarks he does, nevertheless, admit the desirability
of trying to "define the concept" of victimless crimes, and that
this leads him to emphasize the transactional nature of these
activities. Within no more than a few pages, however, he is
compelled to observe that public drunkenness "does not have
the exchange feature focused on here." The trouble is, he is
content to leave it at that.

Surely, we want to know what he thinks of the apparent

contradiction. Does he mean to imply that he does not want us to take too seriously his emphasis on the transactional nature of victimless crimes, because that would exclude public drunkenness and he wants this offense to be counted as victimless? Very well, we will not take his *soi-disant* definition seriously. Or is it his intention to mention public drunkenness as an offense which, though it does not fit his definition and therefore is not a victimless crime, is nevertheless like those activities which do, in that it should be decriminalized just as they should be? Very well, we can accept that. But what we cannot accept is the uncertainty as to which alternative Schur wants, since the two are quite incompatible. The issue here is merely illustrated by the problem of public drunkenness; it has several other instances, as my original discussion showed.

For my own part, I would agree that public drunkenness lacks a transactional nature, and I would also agree that it should be decriminalized. I would assume, however, that Schur would join me in agreeing that some sort of public assistance and treatment must be made available for the drunk, and that in some cases it may have to be imposed on him whether he consents to it or not. The problems here surrounding the proper nature of these constraints and the conditions under which they are appropriate are considerable, as Nicholas Kittrie has shown (Kittrie, 1971, pp. 261–296, especially pp. 293ff.), and they will not go away merely by relieving the drunk of criminal stigmatization. By contrast with this example, consider abortion. Again, always ignoring the status of the fetus, abortion does have the transactional nature which Schur emphasizes, and I also agree with him that it should be decriminalized. But this cannot mean that abortion should be completely unsupervised or unregulated by law, in contrast

to the supply of other similarly dangerous medical services. I
must assume that Schur would agree with me on this, too.

Even this brief discussion shows, to my mind quite conclusively, that Schur's "definition" of the concept of crimes
without victims cannot cover both abortion and public drunkenness; that the main reason why he seems to want it to cover
them both is to be able to advocate decriminalization in both
instances; and that even though both should be decriminalized,
this is no reason for thinking of them as crimes without victims
nor is it any indication that the desirable result of decriminalization should be an unregulated freedom for people to do as
they please.

In this regard, I cannot forbear comment on Schur's vacil-
lation over the best designation for the class of activities he
and others (and, for want of a suitable alternative, I, too)
usually dub "crimes without victims." Schur insists that "the
element of wished-for transaction is the common thread running through the several varying analyses of victimless crime."
Yet he immediately concedes that "there is no gainsaying that
. . . in some ways an alternative concept (such as 'complainantless crime') might more sharply and unequivocally
highlight the key point." If the "key point" is this "common
thread" of transaction, then the term, "complainantless crime"
no more "highlights" it than does "victimless crime." In each
case the connotations requisite to do this are missing. What
is true is that the term "complainantless crime" does at least
have the advantage of covering without distortion both abortion and public drunkenness (to cite only the two examples
discussed above).

The real problem, however, lies elsewhere, and worrying
about the proper name for the class of offenses in question is

in the end no more than an exercise in cosmetics. Changing the name of this class of offenses from "victimless crime" to "complainantless crime" will not affect in the slightest the difficulty I discussed in my original remarks (and which Schur passes over in silence), that no known definition can include all and only those offenses actually discussed under this rubric by Geis, Morris, Packer, Schur and the other authorities in this field. I can only reaffirm my original conclusion in somewhat stronger language: empirical theorists, including my co-author, do not have an adequate conceptual characterization of what they are talking about when they refer to "crimes without victims." Therefore, the sooner this catchy phrase (and its synonym, "victimless crimes") is retired from serious discourse, the better. We can then proceed to talk directly about specific offenses, such as abortion and public drunkenness, and argue the merits of their decriminalization, unhindered by misleading nomenclature and alleged "common threads."

Professor Schur and I agree that the major difference between us is to be seen in our views on how moral principles and sociological facts intersect and how they jointly affect our understanding of the controversy over decriminalization for abortion, gambling, and the rest. The disagreement between us is complicated by Schur's readiness at times to accept some form of moral relativism, and perhaps even of moral subjectivism. Exactly what his views are on normative ethics is a bit obscure, partly because he does not defend his relativism (or subjectivism) except dialectically, that is, as the alternative to what he regards as the inconclusive nature of the objectivist position I defend. In this respect, both of us are handicapped by the recognition that our views of normative ethics are apparently incompatible with each other, and despite our recognition of the importance of this difference to the issues in dispute, neither of us is willing to launch into a full-fledged account of the nature, sources, and validity of moral principles. Under the circumstances, it could hardly be otherwise; the subject simply cannot be disposed of adequately in a few lines or paragraphs.

Far more important to the present discussion, I believe, than these large issues, is the evident disagreement between Schur and me over the adequacy of a purely utilitarian approach to the challenge of overcriminalization and decriminalization. (Perhaps it also should be mentioned here that it is logically impossible to be either a moral relativist or a moral subjectivist and also to believe that the principle by reference to which social policy questions should be settled is one which weighs social goods against social harms. The reason is that such a principle is as objectivist as any moral principle can be.) Although Schur never calls himself a utilitarian, he does protest my criticism of utilitarian reasoning, and he does commit himself to the view that the entire case for decriminalizing abortion, gambling, and the rest, "given the available empirical evidence," rests on the judgment that "such laws [as prohibit abortion, etc.,] appear to be associated with greater social harm than would exist in their absence." Such a judgment is decisive only where the one who makes it accepts, and believes that his audience should accept, the moral principle that basic questions of social policy can be properly settled by weighing the social goods and the social harms which these policies and their alternatives will yield. To think in this way is to be a utilitarian.

Schur is correct that I am not a utilitarian, though he is

incorrect when he implies that I think calculations and estimates of relative social harm are "quite irrelevant." I do think they are relevant, even decisive, but only *after and within* a framework which allows prior recognition to be given to values which are not quantifiable and commensurable in the way social goods and social harms are (supposed to be). Moreover, I think Schur is really closer to me on this than he realizes; either that, or his position verges on a deep inconsistency. Like Mill and the Wolfenden Committee before him, I suspect that Schur does not really adopt, or preserve, a purely utilitarian approach. I have already shown in my initial discussion that Mill, in his appeal to the "intrinsic worth" of "individual spontaneity"—what we might call the underived value of unfettered human self-expression—abandons his professed purely utilitarian approach to the legitimacy of social interference with such self-expression. It simply cannot be true (although Mill seemed oblivious of the fact) that the criterion of value of any social policy lies in its balance of socially good over socially harmful consequences (as any doctrinaire or pure utilitarian must believe) and that there is also intrinsic or underived value in human self-expression (as Mill was eager to insist).

Likewise, when the Wolfenden Committee appealed to a "realm of private morality and immorality," there is the implication that some personal conduct does not affect others, and therefore, such value as it has cannot arise from its social consequences. To put this another way, Mill plainly believed and the Wolfenden Committee probably believed that what gives human freedom its value is not its consequences for social harm or good; if anything, it is the reverse. The very exercise of the free condition or state of persons is itself valuable, and so the value of social policies is to be (at least in part) calculated by reference to whether they enhance or inhibit that self-expression, that value. Schur himself believes this, I think, though he seems unwilling to admit it—or, what is more subtle, unwilling to admit that it matters to his argument for decriminalization. In this connection, Schur's conclusion—that the burden of proof is on those who would restrict individual freedom (including deviance in all its forms), rather than on the advocates of decriminalization (or on both sides with equal weight)—is a revealing symptom of this belief. Why else should those who would use the law to curb deviance have this probative or evidentiary burden?

In my view, therefore, the differences between Mill, Schur, and me are that Mill is an explicit and Schur an implicit utilitarian, whereas I am not a utilitarian at all; that Mill thinks there is no incompatibility between his professed utilitarianism and his acknowledgement of independent value for human freedom, whereas I do (Schur does not seem to confront this issue at all); and that Mill and I avow our belief in the value of human freedom and believe that this value is of fundamental relevance to the controversy over the legislation of morality, whereas Schur does not. Where the three of us do not differ, if I am correct, is in our reliance, tacit with Schur and explicit with Mill and me, on the non-derivative value of human freedom.

Whereas Schur professes to believe that we can establish the rational basis for decriminalization by nothing more than balancing social harm over social good, I think that he has tacitly built into his conception of social goods the value of human freedom. If freedom from no-knock searches and seizures, eavesdropping and entrapment, did not matter so much (and they would not if these freedoms were not fundamental values), then their violation and frustration as a consequence of law enforcement in the "victimless crimes" arena would not matter so much, either. It is the adverse consequences for human freedom in the criminal legislation on morality which we find so objectionable. If this were not so, the costs of over-criminalization would have to be calculated differently, and they could be more cheerfully borne.

It is true, as Schur implies, that there are other social harms and costs which result from using the criminal law to repress vice and deviance, over and above the interferences with freedom. Moreover, some (perhaps Schur among them) would say that these other costs, such as the crime tariff and the causation of secondary criminality, far outweigh in their harmfulness to society the costs resulting from lost freedom. In rejoinder, I would point out two things. First, the truth of this reply to me depends upon large-scale social calculations which have not been, and perhaps cannot ever be, undertaken. Until they are, all persons interested in the outcome of this dispute are obliged to proceed cautiously. Second, the line of argument exhibited in this reply to me cannot get off the ground unless it can persuade us that its basic assumption—that the freedom of some persons is commensurable with (and thus subject to being outweighted and overridden by) harms, costs, and inconveniences for other people—is sound. I do not think that such an approach to human freedom and minority rights is, in the end, rationally defensible. It is, however, a characteristic mark of classic doctrinaire utilitarianism.

I have dwelled on this matter at such length because Schur seems to me, as do most social scientists to most philosophers, to have an inordinate, uncritical attraction for utilitarianism.

He seems not to know, or not to be sobered by the knowledge, that over the past century philosophers have shown how difficult it is for a doctrinaire, single-minded, or unrestricted utilitarianism to explicate and justify our reflective moral judgments. This inadequacy of utilitarianism is nowhere more true and relevant than in the present context. If Schur and I, like Mill before us, did not *care* about individual human freedom for all persons, and if we did not believe, again like Mill, that there is a rational, objective basis (instead of merely arbitrary prejudice, or socially-conditioned attitudes) in support of our conviction, our shared policy outlook against the legislation of morality and in favor of decriminalization would be far less intelligible than it is. In my view, the entire case for decriminalization and all calculations of social cost and benefit are bottomed on an acknowledgement of the value of human freedom, or else they have no foundation at all.

I agree with Schur that a mere appeal to the value of human liberty, and to a doctrine of basic personal rights which gives shape and permanence to the social expression of that liberty, is not likely to find many critics in our society. I concede that those who oppose decriminalization today are not likely to do so by attacking these rights. I also concede that personal rights can conflict, and that these conflicts must be resolved, though I am, it would appear, considerably more optimistic than Schur is about our capacity to resolve such conflicts in a non-arbitrary fashion. I cannot, therefore, share Schur's express reservations about the usefulness of such a doctrine in the present discussion. In my opening statement, I invoked human rights mainly for two reasons. One was to achieve a uniform sense for the idea of being victimized. I find the verdictive or emotive notion of victimization which he has offered in his comments not so much false as irrelevant to this issue. The other reason was to give expression, in political, legal and social controversy, to the incommensurable value of human freedom. I find in his objections no occasion for revising my views on either point.

With regard to my effort to distinguish paternalism from moralism, and to concede some inescapable policy-formation role for the former and at least some explanatory value for the latter, Professor Schur and I seem to be in basic disagreement. I find it little short of amazing that he seems to think there is simply no need at all for concessions to paternalism in the attempt to justify some restrictive regulations which neither he nor I would seek to repeal. Schur's argument for the view that there is no "domain of legitimate paternalism" seems to be in part that the "protective legislation" enacted during the past century to protect women and children is now "condemned as an infringement of their basic rights." (Notice, by the way, that Schur does not hesitate to mention "basic rights" on occasion, and also to use them in his argument as though appeal to them served a useful purpose.) But from the fact that a law was enacted to restrict freedom for a certain class of persons, on the alleged ground that it was for their own ultimate good (and that allegation is subsequently shown to be false), it does not follow that there are no such laws which do what these were originally believed to do. It simply does not follow that, at least in the case of children and some other classes of dependent persons, there are no occasions when for their own good they ought to be coerced by the pressure of law into conduct contrary to what they profess to prefer.

Schur's claim that all such interferences with personal freedom and preference can be "deemed acceptable" on the ground that "they are seen as producing (overall) more good than harm" at best is a confusion of the paternalism of the policies with the justification of that paternalism. (This confusion, incidentally, is simply another consequence of letting utilitarianism, as though it were a universal solvent, obliterate all traces of the operation of other moral principles.) "Good" and "harm" for whom? For the persons whose freedom is restricted, largely. Schur's implication that the good for such persons is considerably outweighed in the balance when compared to the good for everybody else strikes me as quite wrong. Parents force their children to take prudent regard for their own safety in swimming and hiking not mainly because they want to avoid *for themselves* the cost and nuisance of having to pay for hospitalization, but because they do not want their *children* encumbered by the injuries which can result from carelessness and inexperience. The advantage to parents and to society generally weighs very small in the balance when compared to the advantages to the children themselves. The same is true of motorcyclists who are required by law to wear protective headgear. Schur's position, that reform-minded critics need to make no concessions to paternalism, is a major error. It needs only to be mentioned that it is impossible to understand the abortion controversy unless the claims of paternalism are taken seriously. I see little prospect for repeal of all and only the criminal laws which deserve repeal, and which both Schur and I would seek to have repealed, so long as the legitimate claims of paternalism are glibly dismissed.

In this regard, I also must correct Professor Schur's reading of my use of the Prohibition example. He thinks I have cited it to show, in some obscure fashion, "the legitimacy of paternalism." Naturally enough, he views this as "ludicrous." My purpose, however, was nothing like the one he criticizes. I cited Prohibition in order to urge the reader to realize that some efforts to repress vice are not only instances of misguided paternalism; they are also instances of what I called "moralism." In my view, to learn the lesson which the failure of Prohibition teaches requires that we distinguish between paternalism and moralism, and that we realize that even though there is something to be said for paternalism in some situations, a lively awareness of its limitations will not suffice to uproot the legislative enforcement of morality in all cases. To achieve that, an avowed rejection of moralism, too, is necessary. The role of moralism in the entire Prohibition experiment must be acknowledged for its *explanatory* value. This does not, of course, require us to embrace moralism ourselves as a *justification* for such legislation.

Understandably, I am mildly troubled by the fact that Schur seems to have misread my use of the Prohibition example. I am more concerned that he seems to have ignored my distinction between paternalism and moralism and my claim that both are needed to understand the Prohibition controversy. I have, however, no quarrel at all with his remarks that "Prohibition was . . . the classic case of creating, and being unable to enforce, a victimless crime law."

The disagreements between Professor Schur and me—and I have dwelled on them so far to the virtual exclusion of all else—must not be allowed to obscure the substantial areas of agreement which, as he rightly notes, we share. Neither of us has tried to defend current legislative policy which would repress and make criminal abortion, drug offenses, gambling, prostitution, and other such activities. There are to be found spokesmen against legislative reform on these matters, but we are not among them. We agree that legislative and judicial reform, as well as public education and toleration of deviance, is much needed. We also agree that the evidence gathered by social scientists tends overwhelmingly to support the view (which Schur has emphasized rather more than I have) that criminalization of vice, immorality, and deviance will not cause it to go away, and that it will cause more harm than good. There may be students of the empirical evidence who construe it differently or less conclusively than we do; if so, neither of us has any familiarity with their investigations and evaluations. We agree that the burden of restricting human activity where no injuries occur to others falls not on us but on those who defend such restrictions. We also agree that decriminalization is no panacea, and that much hard work in formulating appropriate social policy (with all the trial and error that involves) lies ahead.

With so much to agree upon, it must seem to some unreasonable to have stressed the differences which remain. After all, it is chiefly the policy issues surrounding the toleration of abortion, prostitution, and the rest—issues which Schur and I agree we agree about—that should be the primary focus of attention. If all else is secondary, then emphasis on it runs the risk of serious distortion and may significantly mislead the reader.

Anyone, however, except the utter novice, should know that no serious thinker merely wishes his policy conclusions to be accepted by his audience. In certain settings, for instance, in trying to muster support in a legislative body for repeal of a repressive and dysfunctional criminal law, it may be sufficient to secure agreement solely on the policy issue, and to paper over any disagreements on the rationale behind the vote.

Where such practical circumstances are missing, however, as they are here, then serious advocates are bound to focus most of their energies on trying to make clear and persuasive the method of reasoning they rely upon and on the validity of each of the steps they take in the course of developing their overall argument. The fact that the investigators also agree pretty much on the "yes or no" answer to the policy question is no doubt worth knowing, but it is quite subordinate to other more important considerations.

What matters is the method and the rigor of its use, the concepts and the theory in which they are embedded. Professor Schur and I share agreement on the importance of these matters, especially where as in the present instance we have no power or responsibility to enforce, affirm, change, or nullify any of the law and social policy on abortion, prostitution, and the rest. Our sole job has been to get the issue of overcriminalization and decriminalization, the legislation of morality, the legal control of deviance, in the clearest possible light. The fact that we disagree about how this is to be done is of the utmost importance. The only way that we can advance the argument is to isolate the genuine points of disagreement and bring to them such clarity as we can. This is precisely what we have tried to do.

REFERENCES

KITTRIE, NICHOLAS N., 1971. *The Right to Be Different: Deviance and Enforced Therapy.* Baltimore, Md.: Johns Hopkins University Press.

INDEX